MICHAEL FRAYN

# Copenhagen

*with commentary and notes by*
ROBERT BUTLER

METHUEN DRAMA

**Methuen Drama Student Edition**

10 9 8 7

This edition first published in the United Kingdom in 2003 by
Methuen Publishing Ltd
Reissued with a new cover design and additional material 2009
by Methuen Drama

Methuen Drama
Bloomsbury Publishing Plc
50 Bedford Square
London WC1B 3DP
www.methuendrama.com

Available in the USA from Bloomsbury Academic & Professional,
175 Fifth Avenue/3rd Floor, New York, NY 10010.
www.BloomsburyAcademicUSA.com

ISBN 978 0 4137 7371 5

A CIP catalogue record for this book is available from the British Library

Typeset by Deltatype Ltd, Birkenhead, Merseyside
Printed and bound in Great Britain by
CPI Group (UK) Ltd, Croydon, CR0 4YY

# Contents

# Michael Frayn

1933    8 September: born in North London. He lived first
        in Mill Hill, in a flat above a Victoria Wine Stores.
        His father, Thomas Allen Frayn, was a sales rep for
        Turners' Asbestos Cement, a roofing materials firm.
        His mother, Violet Alice Lawson, studied as a
        violinist at the Royal Academy of Music. She later
        worked at Harrods, where she occasionally modelled
        clothes. The family moved to Ewell, a suburb in
        South London.

1940    Attended 'hideous' private school in Sutton, a
        Dickensian establishment with bullying and beating.

1945    His mother died from a heart attack, aged forty. His
        father had to get a housekeeper and was no longer
        able to afford the school fees. Frayn went to
        Kingston Grammar School. 'It was my good fortune
        to be sent there because it gave me a good
        education.' Frayn swung between being a 'diligent
        little swot who was frightened of everything' and 'an
        obstreperous clown'.[1]

1948    After a brief religious phase Frayn became a
        militant atheist, communist and 'cultural snob'.
        Wrote poetry, stories and plays. As a sixth-former, 'I
        had a very lordly view of life.'

1952    National Service. Trained in Cambridge as a
        Russian interpreter. The playwright, Alan Bennett,
        was on the same course. (They became close friends
        and would later live opposite one another in
        London.)

1954    Attended Emmanuel College, Cambridge, on a state
        scholarship. Read Russian and French in his first
        year and Moral Sciences (Philosophy) for the second
        and third years. His supervisor for his last year,

Jonathan Bennett, recalled: 'I sharply remember his saying at one session – his face expressing a kind of happy earnestness – that when he had read the opening sentence of Wittgenstein's *Tractatus Logico-Philosophicus*, "The world is everything that is the case," it made him "want to dance".[2] Edited *Granta*. Wrote May Week Footlights revue, *Zounds*, which 'fell into the stalls like unrisen sponge cake'.[3] His contemporaries included Frederic Raphael, Bamber Gascoigne, Jonathan Miller and Leslie Bricusse.

1957   Reporter on the *Manchester Guardian*. His beat was the north of England. (He also covered Harold Macmillan's trip to Russia.)

1959   Columnist on the *Manchester Guardian*. His 'Miscellany' column appeared three times a week.

1960   Marriage to Gillian Palmer.

1962   Columnist on the *Observer*. *The Day of the Dog* (articles reprinted from the *Guardian*).

1963   In one column Frayn introduced his famous distinction between ambitious meritocratic 'carnivores' and well-meaning *Guardian*-reading 'herbivores'. *The Book of Fub* (articles reprinted from the *Guardian*).

1964   *On the Outskirts* (articles reprinted from the *Observer*).

1965   In his first novel, *The Tin Men*, computers take over human tasks. Winner of the Somerset Maugham Award. P. G. Wodehouse calls it 'brilliant'.

1966   *The Russian Interpreter*, about a love affair conducted through an interpreter. Winner of the Hawthornden Prize.

1967   *Towards the End of the Morning* ('the only fiction set in Fleet Street that can bear comparison with *Scoop*' Christopher Hitchens). First published in the United States as *Against Entropy*. *At Bay in Gear Street* (articles reprinted from the *Observer*).

1968   *A Very Private Life*, a novel set in the future and written in the future tense. First television play, *Jamie, on a Flying Visit*, broadcast. (The story came to

Frayn in a single sleepless night.)

1969   Second television play, *Birthday*, broadcast.

1970   *The Two of Us* (Garrick Theatre), four one-act
comedies, with Richard Briers and Lynn Redgrave,
attracts hostile reviews. 'All right, they laughed,' said
Frayn of one audience, 'but why didn't they laugh
until they fell helpless on the floor?'[4]

1971   *The Sandboy* (Greenwich Theatre). A newspaper
dispute led to only one review appearing: a
'shattering dismissal' from *The Times*.

1973   *Sweet Dreams*, a novel about a man, waiting at the
traffic lights, who finds himself transported to
heaven – an attractive modern city which offers
unexpected challenges to the modern liberal.

1974   *Constructions*, a non-fiction volume of philosophical
reflections.

1975   *Alphabetical Order* (Hampstead, then Mayfair Theatre),
with Dinsdale Landen and Billie Whitelaw. Winner
of *Evening Standard* Best Comedy Award. An assistant
librarian has an unexpected impact on a provincial
newspaper library. *Imagine a City Called Berlin* (first of
a series of documentaries). Frayn's subjects included
Vienna, Jerusalem, Prague, Budapest and the
London suburbs.

1976   *Donkeys' Years* (Globe Theatre) with Penelope Keith,
about a reunion night at an Oxbridge college. *Clouds*
(Hampstead) with Nigel Hawthorne and Barbara
Ferris (then Duke of York's, 1978) with Tom
Courtenay and Felicity Kendal. A journalist and a
novelist travel round Cuba reporting for rival
magazines.

1978   *Balmoral* (Guildford), a farce set in a royal residence
after the Revolution. 'It was terrible. I withdrew it
and completely rewrote it.'[5]

1979   *Liberty Hall* (Greenwich), the rewrite of *Balmoral*, with
George Cole. Reviews were 'lacklustre'.

1980   *Make and Break* (Lyric, Hammersmith, then Theatre
Royal, Haymarket) with Leonard Rossiter and

Prunella Scales, about a British building components firm at a trade fair in Frankfurt. Winner of *Evening Standard* Best Comedy Award.

1982   *Noises Off* (Lyric, Hammersmith, then Savoy), with Patricia Routledge and Paul Eddington. A farce about actors putting on a farce, it ran for four years.

1983   *The Original Michael Frayn* (articles reprinted from the *Guardian* and the *Observer*).

1984   *Benefactors* (Vaudeville) with Patricia Hodge and Tim Piggott-Smith. The play drew on Frayn's experience when, with his wife and three daughters, he was involved in a housing initiative in Blackheath. (The house was designed and built as part of a small community.) In *Benefactors* an architect finds opposition to his new scheme in unexpected quarters. Winner of four Best Play awards. *Wild Honey*, after Chekhov (Lyttelton, National Theatre) with Ian McKellen.

1986   First screenplay, *Clockwise*, a comedy about a luckless headmaster (John Cleese) en route to give the keynote speech at a head teachers conference.

1989   *The Trick of It*, an epistolary novel about an academic who marries the female novelist who is his main academic subject. Marriage to Gillian Palmer dissolved.

1990   *Look Look* (Aldwych), a farce about audiences, with Stephen Fry as the playwright in Row H of the stalls. Panned by critics, the production ran for 27 performances.

1991   *A Landing on the Sun*, a novel about the death of a civil servant who has been working for the Ministry of Defence.

1992   *Now You Know*, a novel about free-speech campaigners with secrets of their own. The events are narrated in turn through the eyes of each of the eight characters.

1993 *Here* (Donmar), about a couple moving into new accommodation. Married Claire Tomalin, biographer and critic.

1995 *Now You Know* (Hampstead), a play based on his 1992 novel, with Adam Faith. *Speak After the Beep* (articles reprinted from the *Guardian*).

1998 *Copenhagen* (Cottesloe, Royal National Theatre). Winner of *Evening Standard* Best Play of the Year and Critics' Circle awards. *Alarms and Excursions* (Gielgud), short plays and sketches, with Felicity Kendal and Nicky Henson.

1999 *Headlong*, a novel, shortlisted for 1999 Booker Prize. An art historian obsessively pursues a missing Bruegel painting.

2000 *Copenhagen* opens Royale Theatre, New York. Winner of Tony Award (Best New Play). *The Additional Michael Frayn* (articles reprinted from various publications). *Celia's Secret*, co-written with David Burke, a non-fiction account of how David Burke (Bohr in *Copenhagen*) deceived Frayn with forgeries that supposedly related to events in *Copenhagen*.

2002 *Spies*, a novel about two boys during the Second World War. Winner of Whitbread Novel of the Year. Frayn's *Spies* and Claire Tomalin's *The Unequalled Self*, both nominated for Whitbread Book of the Year. (The winner was Tomalin.) Frayn received the Heywood Hill Literary Prize.

2003 *Democracy* (Royal National Theatre).

2007 *The Crimson Hotel* (Donmar Warehouse).

2008 *Afterlife* (Royal National Theatre), based on the life of theatre impresario Max Reinhardt.

[1] www.guardian.co.uk/saturday_review (14 August 1999)
[2] Ibid.
[3] *Observer* (1 April 1984)
[4] Ibid.
[5] *Frayn Plays: Two* (Methuen, 1991), p.viii

# Plot

*Copenhagen* has a non-realistic setting. Three characters exist in an 'afterlife' from which they revisit events in the past. Without any changes in costume or make-up the characters move between periods in their lives. Time and place are fluid as the dialogue locates the action.

*Act One*

The play opens with the Danish physicist, Niels Bohr, and his wife, Margrethe, considering the events that occurred on a single evening during the Second World War. At the time Denmark was occupied by the Germans. In September 1941 the German physicist Werner Heisenberg, a former pupil and colleague of Bohr's, visited the Bohrs' home. Why? The visit was the end of the famous friendship between these two Nobel prizewinners. In the 'afterlife' setting of *Copenhagen*, Heisenberg agrees with the others to make one more attempt to explain his reasons for the trip.

The action flashes back to September 1941. Heisenberg arrives in Copenhagen and Bohr and Margrethe agonise over whether to invite him to their home. Bohr promises not to talk to him about politics but to stick to physics. Heisenberg struggles to remember the details of the trip. As he approaches the house the Bohrs speculate on why he wants to visit them. Bohr welcomes Heisenberg warmly. Margrethe remains detached and sardonic. The pressures of the war make social pleasantries extremely awkward. Heisenberg fails to grasp the depth of the Bohrs' hostility towards Germany. Bohr is half-Jewish. Heisenberg is working for the Nazis as director of nuclear fission research. They all know that the Gestapo are probably monitoring their conversation. Heisenberg asks if Bohr has been in touch with mutual friends, scientists now working in the Allied countries. Bohr resists Heisenberg's advice about staying on good terms with the German Embassy.

The conversation flashes back two more decades to the first time Bohr and Heisenberg met. At the end of one of Bohr's lectures, the twenty-year-old Heisenberg had challenged the famous physicist over his maths. They recall their intense competitiveness, whether they were discussing theoretical physics, playing table-tennis or poker, or skiing. Heisenberg was the quick, impulsive one, Bohr moved slowly and carefully. Heisenberg recalls the headlong manner in which he had met and wooed his wife. There's a momentary silence. Heisenberg knows that the Bohrs are thinking about their children, two of whom died young. Bohr remembers the boating accident in which his eldest son was killed.

Bohr and Heisenberg decide to go for a walk so that they can talk. What Heisenberg has to say is treasonable. As they leave, Margrethe recalls the vast amount of time these two physicists had spent walking and talking. Within ten minutes, the two men have returned. Bohr looks furious and Heisenberg soon leaves. Margrethe wants to know what Heisenberg had to say.

The three of them realise that they cannot agree on the simplest details concerning that evening. Heisenberg says he was asking Bohr if a physicist had the moral right to work on the practical exploitation of atomic energy. Bohr thought Heisenberg was trying to provide Hitler with nuclear weapons. Bohr knew that an explosive chain reaction could never be achieved using natural uranium. Heisenberg knew that uranium could be turned into neptunium, which could be turned into plutonium. At this moment 'the bomb' goes off in Bohr's head.

Heisenberg insists that Bohr had always misunderstood the conversation. He'd told people variously that Heisenberg had tried to pick his brains about fission and the Allied nuclear programme, that Heisenberg was hoping to persuade him that the Germans had no nuclear programme and that Heisenberg had tried to recruit him to work on it. They agree to go over the conversation one more time. They also agree to discuss it in plain language so that Margrethe, a non-scientist, can follow it. Heisenberg says that he tried to explain to Bohr that the future of the atomic bomb lay in the hands of scientists. Both sides would have to desist from building it. What should Heisenberg tell the German government if they came to him asking if it would be possible to produce nuclear weapons? Heisenberg is a patriot. He loves his country. What if the Allies were building an atomic weapon? Bohr says he can tell him nothing about the Allies' programme. Margrethe scorns the suggestion that Bohr should persuade the scientists, driven out of Germany because they were Jews, to stop work on a bomb to defeat Hitler. In September 1941 it looked very likely that Germany would win the war. Heisenberg's scheme would favour the Germans.

Heisenberg says that he didn't try and build the bomb. It wasn't until after the war, when he was detained with other German scientists in a house near Cambridge, that he heard the news about the exploding of an atom bomb. He couldn't believe it. During the war, Bohr worked at Los Alamos, where the atom bomb was developed. Yet after the war, Heisenberg was the one who had to live with thirty years of reproach. Margrethe refuses to let Heisenberg off the hook. She says that he had told the Nazis that he could produce an atomic bomb. Heisenberg insists that when he met with Albert Speer in June 1942 he was able to sideline the atomic project. Bohr scorns the research that Heisenberg had been doing at the end of the war. The three characters agree that after the war their friendship never recovered.

In the silence that follows, the question resurfaces. Why did Heisenberg go to Copenhagen in 1941? They agree to try another draft. For a second time Heisenberg approaches the Bohrs' house. As Bohr opens the door, Margrethe reflects that from these two minds the future will emerge, which cities will be destroyed and which will survive.

## Act Two

We see Bohr and Heisenberg on a walking holiday in Denmark in 1924. These are the early days of their friendship and collaboration. The discussion moves to the three years they spent together working on quantum mechanics, the 'uncertainty principle' and 'complementarity'. By following the discoveries they made in theoretical physics other parallels emerge. Their work led to the realisation that there can be no precisely determinable objective universe. Margrethe challenges their memory of making their discoveries together; in fact the most important ones were made alone. She also points out that the one person you can have no objective view of is yourself. It is therefore no good asking Heisenberg why he came to Copenhagen. Heisenberg's motives, she says, have not always been admirable. Perhaps in returning to Copenhagen he wished to show off his success to his old mentor. Perhaps it was fear of failure that stopped him obtaining large resources from Speer. Later she asserts that Heisenberg didn't build the bomb because he didn't understand the physics. Though Bohr suggests that if Heisenberg had known how close he was he might have made a bomb, Heisenberg maintains that he was never trying to build one. If he wasn't trying to – the question comes up again – why did he go to Copenhagen?

For the third and final time they go through the evening's events. This time round the three characters concentrate on what it was that they were thinking and feeling. Margrethe states that Heisenberg wanted Bohr to understand him and that Bohr's final act of friendship was to leave Heisenberg misunderstood. Heisenberg describes how he survived at the end of the war, when he was nearly shot as a deserter by an SS officer, by offering him a packet of cigarettes. It was a simple solution to a life and death problem. Bohr says that uncertainty and knowledge are inextricable. Heisenberg agrees that the meeting at Copenhagen might have gone a different way and history been very different, there is a final core of uncertainty at the heart of things.

# Commentary

## The playwright's themes

Of the many successful playwrights and novelists working in Britain, some of the playwrights have written a novel and some of the novelists have written a play. Only one writer has achieved notable success in both fields. By 2003 Michael Frayn had written ten novels and fourteen plays, winning literary awards for his novels and theatre awards for his plays. As one reviewer put it, 'Nobody since Chekhov has been as good at both plays and fiction, or as productive.'[1]

How has Frayn achieved this double act? There is only one tip about how to be a successful writer that Frayn has so far volunteered, and that is 'to write the same thing over and over again, changing things very slightly and going on delivering it until people accept it. Very simply, people want reliability and continuity in a writer. If you buy cornflakes you want cornflakes.'[2] When Frayn made this suggestion he was not speaking about his own work. He was referring to more commercially successful novelists whose books are a recognisable brand. No one has ever accused Frayn of writing the same thing over and over again. No one till now, that is.

In fact, Frayn has been praised and censured for doing the opposite. When *Copenhagen* opened at the Royal National Theatre in May 1998 the *Evening Standard*'s theatre critic welcomed the play as 'the most astonishing departure in Frayn's theatrical career'. The *Daily Telegraph*'s critic was not so keen on the change of direction: 'It is impossible not to mourn the fact that Frayn has, temporarily I trust, mislaid his sense of humour.'

As a playwright Frayn had been pigeon-holed in the category marked 'sophisticated light comedy'. He had written the most successful farce of the eighties. In *Noises Off* actors mislay sardines, hide whisky bottles behind radiators and present bunches of flowers to the wrong person. It seems worlds apart from *Copenhagen* in which two physicists discuss neutrons, photons, fission and wave equations. And yet, when these two plays are seen in the context of Frayn's career, evidence can soon be found of reliability and continuity. The subjects and the genres vary wildly but a closer inspection reveals many similar ingredients. Frayn has been following his own advice.

Even before he had the idea of *Copenhagen* we could have listed some themes that we would have expected to see:

- how we shape the world through work
- how we describe the world
- how subjectivity affects that description
- how versions of events conflict
- how memory works
- how we mask our thoughts from others
- how descriptions of events are always subject to rewrites
- how this complexity affects our moral judgements

Frayn's philosophical interest in these questions has been a constant feature of his writing. *Copenhagen* is one more stage in a long line of enquiry that stretches back to Cambridge in the 1950s, if not further still, to his London childhood in the 1940s. Michael Blakemore directed the Royal National Theatre and New York premières of *Copenhagen*. He has also directed six other plays by Frayn. 'I think good writing,' Blakemore says, 'mostly comes out of the preoccupations of a lifetime.'[3]

The spark that first set Frayn thinking about a new subject for a new play, one that would provide a startling and illuminating focus for his interests, came in the mid-nineties when he read a recent book by the investigative journalist Thomas Powers. The title was *Heisenberg's War: The Secret History of the German Bomb*. A hundred pages in, Frayn found his subject.

*Copenhagen* is the story of two physicists who meet for a conversation during the war. After the war neither can agree on what was said. Within this tight framework Frayn investigates questions that he has been considering since he was an undergraduate at Cambridge. These philosophical questions revolve around what we know, feel and think and the uncertain foundations upon which we base these perceptions. In philosophy this area is called epistemology.

As theoretical physicists, Niels Bohr and Werner Heisenberg are involved in unravelling the enigma of the atom. Yet they are unable to agree on basic facts as to what took place during the course of a ten-minute walk. As Bohr's wife, Margrethe, says: 'You reasoned your way, both of you, with such astonishing delicacy and precision into the tiny world of the atom. Now it turns out that everything depends upon these really rather large objects on our shoulders' (p. 76).

The focus in *Copenhagen* narrows down, even further than this, to a particular branch of philosophy known as the epistemology of intention. This examines what we think we are doing and why we think we are doing it. It's a very basic question. The play states it in the opening line. 'But why?' asks Margrethe. Her second line gives the question its context. 'Why did he come to Copenhagen?'

*Copenhagen* concerns the uncertainties that surround motivation. Every actor knows about motivation. It is what actors ask over and over again in rehearsals. Why am I doing this? At drama school actors are often trained to motivate a line of dialogue with a single *action*. The character is doing this or that action because of this or that *objective*. The actors also learn to motivate the *arc* of a character's journey. They do this by thinking of a *super-objective*. The idea underlying this approach is that an audience won't believe in what the character is doing unless the actor believes in what the character is doing. In a well-rehearsed production each line the actor delivers, each move the actor makes, will appear to be logical and intelligible. In this respect, theatre is quite unlike real life, where people are often unable to clarify their objectives, arcs and super-objectives.

Why did one of the world's leading physicists make a particular journey? The answer that Frayn provides in *Copenhagen* takes the audience on a challenging journey of its own. It explores nuclear physics, philosophy and history. For scholars and students each of these academic disciplines has to be approached on its own terms. To discover what goes on inside an atom and what goes on inside the human mind requires separate investigative and analytical skills. A playwright is allowed to take more liberties. A playwright has the licence to play with ideas and subjects and to highlight parallels, analogies and metaphors that fall outside the academic approach to subjects. 'One of the things about the theatre, and fiction, is that you can play,' Frayn told an interviewer. 'You can actually investigate situations that don't exist, and you're not bound by the actuality of the world.'[4]

In *Copenhagen* Frayn plays with the idea of Bohr, Margrethe and Heisenberg meeting up in an 'afterlife' and holding the conversation that they never had during their lives. This situation allows Frayn to combine his interests in philosophy and physics. These two disciplines have been transformed during the twentieth century as our understanding of what goes on inside atoms and what goes on inside the human mind has been revolutionised. More than that, the developments in the first area influenced the developments in the second. Since Frayn explores the relationship between the two in his work, it is worth taking a step back to consider how far-reaching these developments were.

The modern world is often said to have begun in 1905, when the twenty-six-year-old Albert Einstein, a clerk in a patents office in Berne, published 'On the electrodynamics of moving bodies'. This paper became known as the Special Theory of Relativity. Einstein's astonishing revelation was that when one goes at very high velocities (approaching the speed of light), lengths contract and clocks

slow down. Einstein rapidly followed up his discovery with
the quantum theory of light (which proposed that light was
composed of 'wave-packets' called photons), for which he
won the Nobel Prize. That very same year, his research
into Brownian motion provided a powerful argument for
the existence of atoms. Although his work had a profound
effect on the twentieth century, he couldn't possibly have
foreseen what some of these consequences would be.
Einstein was dismayed when he realised that his work had
paved the way for the invention of the atomic bomb. 'It
starts with Einstein,' says Heisenberg in *Copenhagen*. 'It starts
with Einstein,' agrees Bohr (p. 71).

Philosophy had undergone its own revolution in the first
quarter of the twentieth century. In 1911 a young
aeronautical engineer from Vienna had gone to Cambridge
to study mathematics and logic. Three years later he had
to return home to fight in the First World War. During the
war, in which he fought on the Russian and Italian fronts,
Ludwig Wittgenstein completed his masterpiece, the
*Tractatus Logico-Philosophicus* (1922). The book overturned the
way we think about the mind and the body, inner and
outer experience and how we differentiate between our
knowledge of ourselves and others.

In 1929 Wittgenstein came back to teach at Cambridge.
His impact was immense. One area in which he was highly
influential was his analysis of private experience. He
attacked the idea that the mind and the body were
separate entities. He denied that we always know what
mental states we are in. He stated that introspection is not
the same as perception. He could no more look into his
own mind than he could look into the mind of someone
else. Introspection does not grant us a privileged access into
our own minds. Introspection is a form of self-reflection:
'the calling up of memories; of imagined possible situations,
and of the feelings that one would have if . . .'[5]

Wittgenstein's ideas significantly affected the idea of
motive and intention – the theme in *Copenhagen*. If we can
be certain about *what* someone has done and *why* he or she

has done it, we can be fairly confident in describing the
intention and the action as either a good thing or a bad
thing. That's easy enough. But if we don't know exactly
what that person was doing or why they were doing it – or
to take this one stage further – if we can't be sure that
they knew exactly what they were doing or why they were
doing it, we would have to think a lot harder before
describing the intention or the action as good or bad.
Those questions relate to the epistemology of intention.
They lie at the heart of *Copenhagen*.

Wittgenstein died in 1951. Two years later his second
masterpiece, *Philosophical Investigations*, was posthumously
published. One Wittgenstein scholar writes: 'His thought
dominated Anglophone philosophy for the next quarter of a
century.'[6] In 1954 Frayn went up to Cambridge. In his
second and third years he read philosophy. The one book
of philosophy that Frayn has published, *Constructions*, pursues
many of the questions that Wittgenstein raises. It discusses
the nature of perceptions, dreams, memories, love, ambition
and belief. It examines these concepts through elegant
discussions of photographs, toy cars, clouds, animals, Punch
and Judy, Robinson Crusoe, masks, alcoholism, audiences
and writing. In a humorous column he wrote for the
*Observer* Frayn finds himself watching a literary quiz game
on the television. He despairs as he realises how many
books he hasn't read compared to the members of the
panel who appear to have read almost every book that has
been mentioned. His wife cheers him up: 'Anyway, you
know all about all sorts of things they don't. You know
about Wittgenstein, and – well – Wittgenstein . . .'[7]


## The playwright's career

When Frayn was a fifteen-year-old schoolboy at Kingston
Grammar School he wrote poetry and stories. He was also
a communist. His enthusiasm for communism was short-
lived, but his interest in Russia and Russian remained.
(Frayn's Chekhov translations have been highly acclaimed.)

Before he went to university he had to do his National
Service. The fifties was the height of the Cold War, when
British foreign policy was dominated by a deep distrust of
the Soviet Union. Frayn went on a course to train as a
Russian interpreter. It was based at Cambridge and the
recruits wore civilian clothes. The playwright Alan Bennett
was on the same course. Frayn and Bennett became close
friends and put on revues together. Frayn also shared a
billet with someone who was passionate about theoretical
physics and his enthusiasm sparked Frayn's interest. 'If you
study philosophy,' Frayn said, 'you have to be interested in
quantum mechanics, because quantum mechanics has so
many philosophical implications, very difficult implications,
for philosophy.'[8]

The day after he completed his National Service he went
to university – back to Cambridge. As an undergraduate he
wrote a column called 'Saturday Sermon' for *Varsity* and
guest-edited an issue of *Granta*. The writer and broadcaster
Bamber Gascoigne was a contemporary. 'He was almost
exactly the same man then as he is now,' Gascoigne
recalled. 'His quality is as a cool observer and he is
interested in seeing life happening and then turning what
he sees either into humour or drama.' Gascoigne's memory
of Frayn touches on a theme that would surface in
*Copenhagen*. 'He is essentially a thinker and an observer and
if you make too much noise as an observer it kills it as
people start observing you.'[9]

Frayn also wrote the Footlights May Week Revue.
Unfortunately this was the only time the Footlights Revue
didn't go on to the West End. Frayn's disappointment with
the Cambridge Footlights dampened his interest in theatre.
It was only after thirteen years as a journalist and novelist
that he returned to the theatre. His first professional stage
production, *The Two of Us*, was an evening of four short
comedies. In the second of the four, Frayn manages to slip
in a little physics and philosophy. In this one-act play, *The
New Quixote*, Kenneth explains to Gina that he organises his
love life round the principle that nothing is what it seems.

'But it's not just people, you see, Gina. It's everything! It's a general theory for understanding the whole universe! You look at this, and you think, this is a chair. But you look into it more closely and you'll see it's not a chair at all. It's a mass of tiny spinning particles! And what about the particles? Are they really and truly particles? Of course not – they're not particles at all! They're electricity! They're energy! Matter is energy!' 'You're a nut,' replies Gina, 'on top of everything else.'[10]

Frayn had played with scientific and philosophical ideas four years earlier, in his novel *The Russian Interpreter*. There he had raised the problem of reaching any precise measurement of either people or particles. The main character, Manning, has gone on a group expedition to the countryside. In the forest he has been kissed by a beautiful, flirtatious Russian woman called Raya. Manning reflects on what curious organisms human beings are. 'How odd and unfamiliar were the relations between them, like the interactions of half-understood particles beneath the microscope.'[11] The pleasure of the kiss soon mingles with an element of uncertainty. Raya might be a Russian agent. It is a moment that combines three of Frayn's interests: Russia, physics and philosophy.

An idea that concerns both scientists and philosophers is the relationship between the observed and the observer. In physics this is called the Uncertainty or Indeterminacy Principle. In *Copenhagen* Heisenberg explains how a problem arose when what was seen during an experiment didn't match his theory. When an electron was detached from an atom and sent through a cloud chamber it appeared to leave a track. According to quantum mechanics this should not have been possible (p. 65).

In 1927 Heisenberg realised that the track that was visible was not made by the electron but by the collision between the electron and molecules of water vapour. It was the molecules that were leaving the track. 'And that's what we see in the cloud chamber,' Heisenberg says. 'Not a continuous track but a series of glimpses – a series of collisions . . .' (p. 66). By colliding with the electron the molecules also affected the electron's behaviour. This led to one of Heisenberg's major insights: *the instrument of measurement affects that which is being measured.* Heisenberg showed that it wasn't possible to establish the momentum and the position of a particle at the same time.

Frayn uses Heisenberg's Uncertainty Principle in a range of ways in *Copenhagen.* During their wartime meeting both Bohr and Heisenberg know that their conversation is probably being monitored by the Gestapo. When they are in Bohr's house on that September evening their conversation remains circumscribed by the hidden microphone. The observers have changed the behaviour of the observed. On a more general level characters are impossible to describe precisely because they behave differently with different people. In *Constructions* Frayn asks himself why he chooses to be enthusiastic with one person and sceptical with another. He gives the answer that it is the same reason that champagne manufacturers sell dry champagne in England and sweet champagne in America. That's where 'the markets are'.[12]

The hardest person to observe accurately is the one person that we can never see. Ourselves. Any estimation that we make about our own behaviour has to take into account that it is not objective. For this reason our account of our own actions may not necessarily be any more accurate than someone else's account of our actions. As Bohr says about Heisenberg, 'He sees me. He sees Margrethe. He doesn't see himself' (p. 87).

Frayn provides a very funny example of this problem in his novel *Towards the End of the Morning.* A journalist, Dyson, takes part in a discussion programme on TV. Before the show he has a few drinks and during the broadcast he thinks that he is giving a sparkling performance. Later that night he wakes up with an uneasy feeling. The events from the previous evening replay in his mind. In the space of a couple of hours Dyson has gone from thinking his performance was a triumph to realising it was a disaster.

He has swapped one subjective reality for another.[13]

After Cambridge, Frayn joined the newsroom at the *Manchester Guardian*. The cosy atmosphere of newspaper offices in the late-fifties, the rolltop desks, portable typewriters and tea-trolleys, has vanished. The problems of good reporting remain the same today. Frayn's time as a journalist introduces an important theme into his work in general and into *Copenhagen* in particular. This is the subject of language: how the observer chooses to describe the observed. In *Constructions*, Frayn writes, 'Language is not the world talking about itself. Language is you talking to me about the world.'[14]

During the 1960s Frayn had won a reputation as a journalist and novelist. In the mid-1970s he established himself as a playwright. After *The Two of Us* Frayn wrote *The Sandboy*, which flopped. And then, in the space of two years, three full-length plays appeared: *Alphabetical Order* (1975), *Donkeys' Years* (1976) and *Clouds* (1976). The third one directly addresses the subject of journalism. In *Clouds*, a newspaper reporter, Owen, finds to his dismay that he has to travel round Cuba with Mara, a female novelist. Owen explains to Mara how the demands of his job are quite unlike the demands of hers. 'Proper reporting involves getting quotes down accurately. Spelling names right. Checking. Then checking again. Boring, meticulous skills that you don't learn by writing fiction. It also involves coming face to face with the real world, a very muddled and overcrowded place where nothing has its name on it, and everything is somehow the wrong shape to be expressed in language.'[15]

In *Copenhagen* Niels Bohr insists that everything has to be expressed in plain language. 'You know how strongly I believe that we don't do science for ourselves,' Bohr says, 'that we do it so that we can explain to others . . .' (p. 38). 'Plain language, plain language!' Heisenberg reminds Bohr, when Bohr uses the phrase 'indeterminate recoil' (p. 68). Science does not lend itself readily to plain language. Bohr once said that in important questions, one might speak clearly or accurately, but never both, and neither easily.[16]

It is no easier for writers. 'When you have to describe some real thing,' Frayn told an interviewer, 'it always turns out to be hideously complicated. Nothing will tie together. It won't make a story. It won't make a plot. It won't tie up. And that is the difficulty of the world from the point of view of the writer. It's not in words. It's tree-shaped and cloud-shaped and room-shaped. It's not word-shaped.'[17]

After two years on the *Guardian*, Frayn took over its 'Miscellany' column, which appeared three times a week. In 1962 he moved to the *Observer* where he wrote a column for six years. His columns included pastiches of nature notes, election broadcasts and childcare manuals, satires of fashionable attitudes and comic transpositions in which modern manners were placed in an historical context. Frayn's journalism also revealed an affection for the overlooked aspects of everyday life. As he put it, 'the really basic stuff'.[18] For instance, Frayn liked home movies, slides and holiday snapshots. In an article titled 'Private Collections' he praises the 'modesty of snapshots – the fact that they make no claims, imply no principles, demand no reactions'. Frayn quotes an observation of Wittgenstein's from the *Tractatus*: 'The mystical thing is not *how* the world is, but *that* it is.'[19] These snapshots, Frayn writes, show us that 'things are what they are, and that they are significant in themselves, for their own sake'.

Thirty years later Frayn returned to this theme in his novel *Headlong*. The narrator, Martin Clay, tells a neighbour about the book he is writing. His subject is a group of medieval painters in the Netherlands who had been influenced by 'nominalism'. They liked the really basic stuff too. Clay explains that these painters placed tremendous concentration upon 'individual, ungeneralised objects, on things that offer themselves not as indications of abstract ideas, but as themselves, as nothing more nor less than what they are'.[20]

In another *Observer* column titled 'In the Superurbs', Frayn confesses to the reader that 'For a long time now

I've nursed the vague project of writing a guide-book to my
native London suburbs'. Frayn has the idea of 'actually
*describing* the suburbs, without either laughing at them or
moralising about them'.[21] Frayn did make a celebrated
documentary about the suburbs. He has a keen sense of
*milieu*, the mental atmosphere that thrives in a particular
time and place. He has also made documentaries about
two cities, Vienna and Berlin, that were hothouses of
intellectual, artistic and political thought. In the
introduction to *Towards the End of the Morning*, Frayn says
that Fleet Street was a place which was also 'a way of life
with its own style and philosophy'.

It is characteristic that in *Copenhagen*, as in his
documentaries, Frayn's instinct is to describe the complexity
of the subject rather than to moralise about it. After
*Copenhagen* had opened in London and on Broadway, Frayn
gave a lecture to the Royal Society in London. 'I didn't
really want to get into the morality of atomic weapons,' he
told his audience, 'I wanted to get into the question of how
we know why we do what we do. We can't come to any
moral judgements of people or ourselves until we can make
some estimation of motivations. The difficulties of doing
this points to a fundamental difficulty in making moral
judgements.'[22]

To make some estimation of motive you need to know
the facts and people frequently disagree about facts. In
*Copenhagen* Margrethe challenges Bohr about the way that
he remembers the past. Margrethe thinks he turns it into a
story: 'it all falls into place, it all has a beginning and a
middle and an end.' When her memory takes her back,
what she sees is confusion, rage, jealousy, tears and 'no one
knowing what things mean or which way they're going to
go' (p. 73). For Margrethe, the sheer amount going on was
appalling. This is a major theme in Frayn's work. The first
entry in his book of philosophy, *Constructions*, states it clearly.
It is also reproduced in large type on the book's back cover.

[1] The complexity of the universe is beyond expression in any
possible notation.

> Lift up your eyes. Not even what you see before you can ever be
> fully expressed.
> Close your eyes. Not even what you see now . . .

The point is, there's just so much out there. The way we
deal with this overabundance is to filter, classify, narrate,
organise, arrange, prioritise and label. It's a full-time job.
As Lucy, the resident librarian in *Alphabetical Order*, says,
'I'm worn out with the sheer hard labour of seeing any
sense in anything.'[23]

There is a philosophical theory about the nature of facts,
developed by Bertrand Russell and Wittgenstein, called the
doctrine of logical atomism. In this theory everything gets
broken down to its irreducible constituents. The empirical
essence of this theory is stated by Wittgenstein in the first
proposition of the *Tractatus*: 'The world is everything that is
the case.' In *Alphabetical Order* a rumpled, erudite journalist,
John, visits the library and challenges this idea. Newspapers
appear every day. Readers are presented with more events,
more stories, more facts. 'At each moment more and more
is the case, so that if the world is everything which is the
case, then the world is in a state of continuous expansion,
or perhaps, more properly in a state of continuously
increasing logical density.'[24]

A newspaper is one way we control the flow of
experience. Memory is another. Frayn's next play, *Donkeys'
Years* takes place on an Old Boys' reunion at an Oxbridge
College. It is a companion piece to *Alphabetical Order*: one
deals with how we consciously interpret the world, the
other with how we unconsciously interpret it. In *Donkeys'
Years* men in their forties return to the scene of their
student days, drink vintage port and recall their youth.
They remember events as if it were yesterday. The MP,
Christopher Headingley, says, 'I feel as if I'd never been
away.'[25] The way that the past and the present coexist is a
theme in *Copenhagen*:

> **Bohr**  A curious sort of diary memory is.
> **Heisenberg**  You open the pages, and all the neat headings and

tidy jottings dissolve around you.

**Bohr**  You step through the pages into the months and days themselves.

**Margrethe**  The past becomes the present inside your head. (p. 6)

Memory can be unreliable as it skips, selects and blurs. An event's significance is not reflected in the quality or quantity of what is remembered. Our memories can only be partial recollections of what one person thought was happening. In *Clouds* the journalist and the novelist travel round Cuba with an American academic and a local guide. During the day they bump along dusty tracks looking at sugar mills and fertiliser plants. In the evenings the sound of typewriters mixes with the sound of cicadas. The guide presents one version of Cuba, Owen and Mara write up two others. They are both writing pieces for rival Sunday supplements. (These were the days when there were only two Sunday supplements.) Owen suggests that they find some way of dividing up the material between them. Mara sees no need: 'The clouds you see aren't the clouds I see.'[26]

When Heisenberg meets Bohr in September 1941 he has to be very careful about what he says in case their conversation is monitored. 'I think you must assume that you and I aren't the only people who hear what's said in this house.' They go out for a walk. They still can't be sure that they won't be overheard. Heisenberg has to speak to Bohr that evening about an extraordinarily delicate and dangerous matter. To discuss nuclear research was an act of treason. So he phrases what he says in a tantalisingly vague way. 'I didn't say anything about anything!' says Heisenberg. 'Not in so many words. I couldn't!' (p. 36). In effect, he presents Bohr with something distinctly cloudy. The tragedy is that they do not see the same cloud.

Frayn's plays have plenty of empty spaces. There is the blue sky in *Clouds*. 'Cuba' reads the opening stage direction in *Clouds*. 'Or, at any rate, an empty blue sky.' There are the blank pages that roll through Owen's and Mara's typewriters and the blank pages in *Copenhagen* on which the three characters try to work out what happened. 'One more draft, yes?' (p. 86). There is the empty room in Frayn's play *Here*. The opening stage direction reads 'bare floor, bare walls, no furniture'. This is the room which a youngish couple, Cath and Phil, have to decide whether or not to rent. If they choose it, this is where their lives will unfold. Emptiness stimulates the imagination. In *Benefactors* the architect, David, tells his neighbour about the best part of his job, 'I'll tell you what's really magical. A bare building site . . . Amazing emptiness, like the emptiness of a conjuror's hat, because you know that marvels will come out of it.'[27] A cloudless sky, a blank page, a bare building site, an empty room and a conjuror's hat: these are all full of possibilities. They are points of departure. In the final line of *Clouds* Mara looks up at the sky and sees a new beginning: 'Not a cloud in sight. Pure light. Pure emptiness. Everything.'

These empty spaces present a challenge to Frayn's characters, who strive to fill them. In *Benefactors* David is designing two tower blocks. He has been persisting with this frustrating building project in the face of considerable opposition. 'Because if I can get these two towers up that will be something fixed. Two pieces of space will have an outline . . . They won't melt into different shapes.'[28] His work as an architect allows him to shape the world around him. Frayn has written about librarians in *Alphabetical Order*, academics in *Donkeys' Years*, journalists in *Clouds*, salesmen in *Make and Break*, actors in *Noises Off*, an architect in *Benefactors* and free-speech activists in *Now You Know*. 'I like to write about people doing real jobs,' he said in an interview. 'Too many dramatists write about characters who are idling, whose engines are not connected to the road.'[29]

These real jobs share a common quality. They all involve interpreting the world and giving it a shape. Take the example of the salesman. He isn't selling a product, he is selling the perception of a product. 'These are not brushes, madam, they're eco-friendly, fuel-efficient cleansing tools.'[30] If there is a single group that, perhaps more than any other, has changed the way the modern world is interpreted and shaped, it is scientists: the ones doing the real jobs in *Copenhagen.*

## Background to the play

Imagine a city of 250,000 people. On a clear sunny August morning the city's inhabitants are finishing breakfast, glancing at the paper, hurrying out of the home to go to work or to school. It is nearly 8.15. A minute later a pinkish light bursts in the sky and more than half the city is destroyed. Eighty thousand people are killed instantly. Tens of thousands more die from the effects of the explosion. Two minutes later, the pilot of the plane that has dropped the bomb looks down from 33,000 feet. 'Where before there had been a city,' he recalled, 'with distinctive houses, buildings and everything that you could see from our altitude, now you couldn't see anything except a black boiling debris down below.'[31]

It is a grim irony that the exhilarating discoveries made by physicists in the first four decades of the twentieth century led to Hiroshima on 6 August 1945. The uranium 235 fission bomb that exploded over the eighth largest city in Japan had the impact of 20,000 tons of TNT. The fireball was almost 110 yards in diameter. Two days later, Radio Tokyo ended its first full report by saying that the United States had used methods which 'have surpassed in their hideous cruelty those of Genghis Khan'.[32] The Americans had only recently got hold of the method of 'hideous cruelty' that would end the war. If a handful of physicists had been working for other countries, or the physicists in other countries had made other calculations, this bomb might have been in other hands and have exploded over other cities. 'London, presumably,' as Bohr says to Heisenberg, 'if you'd had it in time' (p. 84).

How did the Americans get there first? The quickest answer takes us back two and a half years to the desert of New Mexico, USA. In the early 1940s a boys' private school was converted into a massive science laboratory. The location had been chosen because it was sparsely populated, it was away from the sea, and it had a reasonable year-round climate. This was to be the main part of a massive industrial, technical and scientific programme called the Manhattan Project. The school became the centre for the development of the bomb. In the early forties Los Alamos became a self-contained town with barbers' shops, laundries and gas stations. Carpenters, metalworkers and plumbers moved in. In February 1943 the scientists arrived. Many were refugees from Nazi Germany. As Margrethe says, 'The Germans drive out most of their best physicists because they're Jews. America and Britain give them sanctuary. Now it turns out that this might offer the Allies a hope of salvation' (p. 45). The influx of Jewish scientists from Germany has been called 'Hitler's Gift'. The converted school was filled with an extraordinary intellectual buzz. One scientist spoke of Los Alamos as having 'a spirit of Athens, of Plato'.[33] It was an academy with a daunting sense of purpose. This was spelt out in one group of lectures collected in *The Los Alamos Primer*. 'The object of the project is to produce a practical military weapon in the form of a bomb. . .'[34] Many scientists went to Los Alamos with the specific aim of working on a bomb that would defeat Hitler. Regrettably, it was never going to be possible to drop an atom bomb on a single person. After Niels Bohr escaped from Denmark in 1943 he also went to work at Los Alamos. Heisenberg challenges him that the plan was to drop an atom bomb on the Germans. 'You were dropping it on anyone who was in reach . . . my fellow-countrymen. My wife. My children. That was the intention. Yes?' Bohr replies, 'That was the intention' (p. 43).

This aim ceased on 30 April 1945 when Hitler committed suicide. On 7 May Germany surrendered and the war in Europe was over. But that was only half of the war. As one historian neatly summarises it: 'Two separate wars made up the "Second World War": a European war and a Far Eastern war. After 1941 the United States and the United Kingdom took part in both, while their enemies waged separate wars.'[35] With Germany's surrender, all attention switched to the Far East.

Before Hitler's suicide a number of Allied scientists had signed a petition that was sent to the American President asking that the atomic bomb never be used. The petition was disregarded. The scientists were not in control of their research. Senior Allied strategists had known for several years that they would need the bomb to defeat Japan and to defy Russia. The ethics of bombing had changed during the six years of the war from an early position, when it was considered wrong to bomb civilians or private property, to a later position, when German and Japanese cities were mercilessly bombed in an attempt to destroy each nation's morale. On 16 July, at the Trinity site in New Mexico, the Los Alamos scientists successfully exploded the first atom bomb. The explosion could be seen from 180 miles away. Its significance was not lost on those present. The director of the test, Kenneth Bainbridge, said, 'Now we're all sons of bitches.' The man in charge of the Los Alamos project, J. Robert Oppenheimer, quoted from *Bhagavad-Gita*, 'I am become Death, destroyer of Worlds.'[36] Its significance was not lost either on those who soon heard about it. The American President Harry S. Truman noted in his diary, 'It seems to be the most terrible thing ever discovered, but it can be made the most useful.'[37]

The Potsdam Conference took place over the next fortnight. Churchill, Truman and Stalin were meeting to discuss plans for the post-war world. Churchill noticed a decisive change in the American President's manner. When Churchill learnt of the test in New Mexico he realised the reason for Truman's behaviour. 'He told the Russians just where they got off,' Churchill observed, 'and generally bossed the meeting.'[38] America had seen the future. Three weeks after the test explosion, the first atomic bomb was dropped on Hiroshima. Three days later, a second bomb was dropped on Nagasaki. Japan surrendered immediately.

The bombs ended the war and changed the way post-war generations perceived the world.

In Britain, 6 August was a bank holiday. It had been a day of sunshine and thunderstorms. A record crowd at Lords had seen Australia make 273 for 5 wickets.[39] The nine o'clock news on the BBC began: 'Here is the news. It's dominated by a tremendous achievement of Allied scientists – the production of the atomic bomb.' The announcer went on to say, 'There's no news yet of what devastation was caused.' Among those listening to the broadcast was a group of German scientists. They had been captured at the end of the war and spirited back to Britain to keep them out of the hands of the Russians. They were kept as detainees in Farm Hall, a country house near Cambridge. This group included Nobel prizewinners, Nazis and non-Nazis. The scientists were stunned by the announcement on the BBC. When they first heard the news they thought it was a hoax. 'We sit up half the night,' Heisenberg tells Bohr, 'talking about it, trying to take it in. We're all literally in shock.' (p. 46).

What these scientists didn't realise was that their conversations were recorded. The British secret service had installed microphones in the rooms and transcripts of the conversations were regularly typed up and sent to officials in London and Washington. Nearly fifty years later the Public Record Office in Kew released the transcripts. It was now possible to follow the scientists' thoughts as they discussed how an atom bomb might be built. The transcripts made clear exactly how close the German scientists had got to building an atom bomb. They were nowhere near. The transcripts raise a number of questions. Did the Germans not build the bomb because they thought it could not be done or because they tried to build it and failed? Or did they refrain from making the attempt? This last question raises two further ones. Did they consciously sabotage any efforts to build the bomb or did they merely lack the zeal to pursue the science because, subconsciously, they didn't want to?

Thomas Powers, the author of a Pulitzer Prize-winning book about the CIA as well as books that cover the Vietnam War and National Security, was one of the first historians to make use of the Farm Hall transcripts. In 1993 he published *Heisenberg's War: The Secret History of the German Bomb*. Powers was not the first person to write about Heisenberg, but he emerged as one of the most sympathetic. He set out to answer the question: why had Nazi Germany failed to build an atom bomb? In 1939, the Germans had been well ahead. 'Nuclear fission had been discovered in Germany,' Powers wrote, 'Europe's only uranium mines were controlled by Germany, and in May 1940 German armies seized the world's only heavy-water plant, in Norway.'[40] According to Heisenberg's biographer, David Cassidy, 'The German research effort seemed poised for early success in the autumn of 1941.' Heisenberg himself said, 'It was from September 1941 that we saw an open road ahead of us, leading to the atom bomb.'[41] What happened?

Frayn read Powers' 'wonderful' book soon after it was published and came across the story of Heisenberg's trip to Copenhagen to meet Bohr. Accounts of this visit had appeared in other books, but Frayn read about it here. 'The problem is that there is no agreement about what was actually said,'[42] Powers writes, adding four pages later, 'The two versions of the conversation reported that night . . . could hardly have been more different.' The exact purpose of Heisenberg's visit has never been clear. Powers' description of the meeting appealed to Frayn for its philosophical implications. 'I immediately thought that this crystallises the whole problem of knowing why people do what they do,' Frayn said, 'because there is this very practical question about a really quite striking event.'[43]

Heisenberg was a patriot, he was not a Nazi. He knew that it would be disastrous to develop a bomb that Hitler could use. He also knew that the Americans might be driven to invent the bomb out of fear that the Germans would get there first. It was his colleague Carl Friedrich von Weizsäcker who suggested that Heisenberg visit his old mentor, Niels Bohr, and discuss the situation. Heisenberg had a 'vague hope' that the international community of scientists might agree to halt the development of the atomic bomb. Two years earlier his plan would have stood a better chance. As Heisenberg later said, 'In the summer of 1939, twelve people might still have been able, by coming to mutual agreement, to prevent the construction of atomic bombs.'[44]

On Monday 15 September 1941 Heisenberg arrived in Copenhagen. He had a lecture to give on the Friday evening. On Wednesday night he met – very probably went to dinner – with Bohr. It was a fraught occasion. In the two chapters in *Heisenberg's War* that deal with this event Powers shows how an ambition of far-reaching significance foundered because neither person began to understand the other. Bohr's suspicion of Heisenberg's motives prevented him from seeing Heisenberg's point of view. Heisenberg's underestimation of Bohr's anti-Nazi feeling made conversation almost impossible.

The situation was remarkable: a man attempts to halt the development of the atom bomb and fails because he cannot make himself understood to a highly intelligent man who knows him extremely well. An unbridgeable gap existed between the reason Heisenberg thought he was making the visit and the reason Bohr thought Heisenberg was making the visit. This is the psychological confusion at the heart of Powers' description. It is a story about indeterminacy in which the main character is the man who invented the Principle of Indeterminacy. 'If I hadn't been interested in indeterminacy,' Frayn recalled, 'and hadn't been interested in human motivation, it probably wouldn't have helped to have read that story.'[45]

What did Heisenberg hope to achieve from this meeting? It was never clear. Perhaps he wanted Bohr to acknowledge that the physics was possible. Or he wanted Bohr to accept that Heisenberg was right to continue working on the project. Or he wanted Bohr to speak to the scientists

working for the Allies. Or he simply wanted Bohr's
absolution. No one knows. No one knows if Heisenberg
really knew. It was the situation's opaqueness that appealed
to Frayn. 'It suggested a way of coming at various
problems I had been thinking about for many years in
human motivation,' Frayn said. 'Why people do what they
do. Why one does what one does oneself.'[46] For Frayn,
reading Powers' book had been a piece of luck. But luck
itself has its own rationale. As Frayn told one interviewer,
'All luck is usually a combination of external circumstance
and some sort of internal situation.'[47]

The advances in physics had created many problems for
philosophers. But the advances in physics also created many
philosophical problems for physicists as they found
themselves facing extraordinary ethical dilemmas. 'It is one
of the great ironies of nuclear physics,' Frayn told an
interviewer, 'that when it began, it was a subject, like
theology or Egyptology, with no practical application. It's
almost impossible to imagine your way back to that world:
it's like the story of the Garden of Eden.'[48]

Scientists had belonged to a remarkably open
international community. They studied in each other's
countries. They attended conferences, published papers and
followed up on each other's breakthroughs. Niels Bohr
catches this innocence early in *Copenhagen*: 'Heisenberg is a
theoretical physicist. I don't think anyone has yet
discovered a way you can use theoretical physics to kill
people' (p. 10). Physics had always attracted highly
competitive people. Bohr and Heisenberg were highly
competitive about most things: from skiing and table-tennis
to poker. Physics could never have made the progress that
it did if physicists had not been intensely aware of each
other's work. Before the war the prize they were after was
the Nobel. During the war, the prize they were after was
victory. All the rules had changed.

When Fritz Strassmann and Otto Hahn achieved fission
in 1939 they published the breakthrough in the journal
*Nature*. The screenwriter Bruce Robinson, who wrote *The*

*Killing Fields* and *Withnail and I*, also wrote the screenplay
*Fat Man and Little Boy* about the American atomic
programme. 'If you're about to start a war,' says Robinson,
'and you're looking for a nuclear weapon it's not too smart
to put what you've discovered in an international science
magazine.'[49] When the war broke out, scientists realised
that science, which had always been based on the speedy
dissemination of knowledge, had now become steeped in
secrecy. 'You discover penicillin and within five minutes the
information is everywhere,' says Robinson. 'It isn't like that
any more, and The Bomb is one of the reasons it isn't.
That's where all this stuff started, keeping discoveries
secret.'[50]

## Play v. novel

Frayn is often asked how he decides if an idea is a play or
a novel. The answer he gives in the Introduction to *Plays: 3*
is that 'the matter decides itself'. In a novel the reader has
access to the private and unspoken thoughts of the
characters. In a play, Frayn writes, 'One sees only as much
of each person as he or she chooses to reveal – or fails to
keep concealed.' In an interview Frayn states this principle
from another angle. 'I think the crucial difference is that
it's very natural in the novel to be inside the head of a
character, or all the characters if you like. In the theatre,
it's most natural to be outside the head of the characters.
Again, you can have characters talk about their thoughts,
soliloquise, address the audience directly. But the natural
mode of theatre is dialogue.'[51] Frayn knew *Copenhagen*
needed an audience. It was essential to the story, to the
way he wanted to tell it, and to the answer to its riddle.
One clue to the motive behind Heisenberg's visit can be
found in *Constructions*, where Frayn wrote: 'You're a cloud,
and you rely on me to see a face in you.'[52]

   At first Frayn had thought of writing about the scientists
while they were detained and closely monitored at Farm
Hall. 'The story of Farm Hall is another complete play in

itself' (see Postscript, p. 115). He also thought of having
other actors playing characters who were listening to the
three characters when they were meeting in Copenhagen in
1941. 'I knew that both men would probably be under
surveillance by the Gestapo, and Heisenberg was certainly
under surveillance by British Intelligence later on. So I
thought I would have the Gestapo and the British
Intelligence listen in on the conversations and tell the
audience what was going on. But then gradually I thought
"do we need these people? Do we need these extras just
sitting in in the darkness listening to what's happening.
We've got an audience already, why not use them?" So in
the end that's what I've done. I've made the audience who
sat in the theatre the audience for the conversations of
Bohr and Heisenberg.'[53]

In 1990 Frayn had written *Look Look*, a play about an
audience. The stage showed the cross-section of the stalls,
with a dozen members of the audience, an usherette and a
playwright watching the playwright's play. 'Really what
*Copenhagen* is about is what *Look Look* is about,' Frayn told
me. 'It's about audiences. It's why in *Copenhagen* we have
the audience right around the stage. To know what you're
thinking yourself, you need a reaction from other people.
That's why, in the end, Heisenberg goes to Copenhagen.
To have an audience.'[54]

*Look Look* offers its own stark example of the gap between
what one group thinks it is doing and what another group
makes of it. 'I remember with *Look Look*,' Frayn said,
'everyone in rehearsals thought it was wonderful. Michael
Codron [the producer] came to the last run-through in the
rehearsal room and I said, "What notes have you got?" He
always has lots of scratchy notes. And he said, "None.
Marvellous. Wonderful." And we got in front of the first
preview audience at the Aldwych and we all knew it was
dead. There was no way we were ever going to breathe life
into that corpse.'

After six weeks' rehearsing *Copenhagen* the cast at the
National were saying that what they needed now was an

audience. They needed to find out what it was they were doing. 'That's just what the play's about!' Frayn told the *Copenhagen* cast. 'Heisenberg was seeking an informed sympathetic audience, for whom he had done plays before, as it were. To try out this play.'[55]


## Heisenberg and the Nazis

Heisenberg's biographer, David Cassidy, posed a large and testing question about Heisenberg's behaviour before and during the war:

> How was it possible that Werner Heisenberg, one of the most gifted of modern physicists, a man educated in the finest tradition of Western culture, who was neither a Nazi nor a Nazi supporter, how was it possible that such a man would not only choose to remain in National Socialist Germany for its entire twelve years of existence, but also actively seek a prominent academic position in Berlin at the height of the war, a position that included the scientific directorship of nuclear fission research for the German Army at war?[56]

It's a question, obviously, that is asked in hindsight. When considering Heisenberg's actions we have to remember to distinguish between what he knew at the time and the full horrors of the Nazi regime that emerged at the end of the war. We also need to remember what he knew and what he might have been able to do about what he knew. There was always the hope, among many Germans, that the virulent anti-semitism would subside, that the Hitler hysteria would blow over, or that Hitler would be deposed or assassinated. (There were thirty-one attempts on Hitler's life.) The position for many 'good Germans' was that they wanted Germany to win the war and Hitler to lose it. During this period their loyalties were torn. 'It would be another easy mistake to make,' says Heisenberg in *Copenhagen*, 'to think that one loved one's country less because it happened to be in the wrong' (p. 42).

But we also have to remember the nature of the events

that were unfolding in Germany in the 1930s and 1940s. Heisenberg would certainly have witnessed the national boycott of all Jewish shops on 1 April 1933. He would have known about the burning of hundreds of thousands of 'un-German' books (including ones by Einstein, Freud and Thomas Mann) in thirty cities around Germany on 10 May 1933. He would have known about the introduction of the Nuremberg Laws, which relegated Jews to second-class citizenship on 15 September 1935. He would have known about the looting of 7,000 Jewish shops, the burning of hundreds of synagogues and the arrest of 20,000 Jews on Kristallnacht, the night of broken glass, on 9 November 1938.

Heisenberg knew that his Jewish colleagues were barred from posts. Many colleagues had left the country. As the war progressed he knew that colleagues and relatives of colleagues had been sent to concentration camps. During his captivity in Farm Hall after the war ended he admitted this to another of the detainees. Yet Heisenberg still went on trips abroad, as a cultural ambassador for his country, and worked as scientific director of nuclear fission research. By any standards he was severely compromised.

Some distinguished Germans actively endorsed the efforts of the Nazis. In May 1933 Germany's most distinguished philosopher, Martin Heidegger, spoke encouragingly of German students committing themselves to the service of the *völkisch* state. In June 1934 Hitler ordered the murder of his enemies within the Nazi party in the 'Night of the Long Knives'. A law was subsequently issued that legitimised the murders. The country's leading constitutional lawyer, Carl Schmitt, published an article in support of these steps that was (unbelievably) titled 'The Führer Protects the Law'.

There were many prominent figures in German cultural life who never endorsed the Nazis' actions. The charge that is still made against these figures is that they lent legitimacy to the Nazi regime by not leaving the country or actively opposing it. For instance, in his biography of Hitler, Ian

Kershaw writes that the composer Richard Strauss and the conductor Wilhelm Furtwängler 'continued to bestow distinction on German achievements in music'.[57]

The issue of how educated, apparently 'decent' Germans carried on working in Nazi Germany has become a subject of increasing fascination for British dramatists. Their interest in these grey areas of ambiguity, contradiction and divided loyalty has been fuelled by substantial new works of scholarship. Michael Burleigh's recent book *The Third Reich* takes as its central theme 'this assault on decency'. In his introduction Burleigh notes 'a growing interest in the choices made by individuals of the time, with compelling new biographies of Heidegger, Heisenberg or Speer, among the major figures'.[58] Burleigh mentions Gitta Sereny's biography of *Albert Speer: His Battle with Truth* and Powers' *Heisenberg's War*. David Edgar's play *Albert Speer* is based on Sereny's book, which also inspired Harold Pinter's play *Ashes to Ashes*. Powers' book on Heisenberg inspired *Copenhagen*. Burleigh also cites two important new biographies about Heidegger. Perhaps the next play about the moral choices made by a brilliant German in the thirties will centre on this controversial philosopher.

The question that each of these subjects poses is twofold. One: what exactly did he do? Two: what would we have done? Plays do not set out to present characters as either good examples that we should emulate or bad examples that we should avoid. In his Afterword to *Albert Speer* David Edgar writes that the response most great drama demands of us is neither 'yes, please' nor 'no thanks' but 'you too?'. It is a version of 'there but for the grace of God go I'.[59] As we watch these characters on stage we identify with their predicaments. Most of us will never have to face moral choices of this magnitude. It is unlikely that most of us would behave as heroes. The chances are that we would look for a compromise, a way out, a balance between what we ought to do and what we think we can do. As Frayn writes about Heisenberg, 'Why shouldn't he try to juggle principle and expediency, as we all do?' (p. 138).

The subject of the 'good German' is explicitly explored in C. P. Taylor's play *Good*, where we see an ostensibly decent man, Halder, an academic, husband, father – gradually become a Nazi. *Good* explores, in Taylor's words 'how a "good" man gets caught up in the nightmare of the Third Reich'.[60] The strength of the play lies in making the gradual shifts from an understandable position to an utterly malign one appear barely perceptible.

The architect Albert Speer was as active in promoting Hitler's cause as it was possible to be. Even he claimed not to know what exactly was going on. David Edgar's play *Albert Speer* shows how Hitler's favourite architect, and later his Minister of Armaments, managed to conceal from himself the full horror of what was happening in his country. Speer would see crowds of people waiting for evacuation on the station platform. 'But he'd never speculated,' says Pastor Casalis, who became his confessor figure, 'what would happen to them at the other end.'[61] In the play's climax Speer confronts the possibility that what he had always believed about his own life (that he never knew what was going on) was a lie. Speer says, 'If I "turned away", I knew.'[62]

There was a strong desire not to know: to keep your head down, protect your family, career, and – when possible – help colleagues. In Ronald Harwood's play *Taking Sides*, Furtwängler, conductor of the Berlin Philharmonic Orchestra, is cross-examined immediately after the war. Furtwängler's compromises were not untypical. He helped Jewish members of his orchestra. He also conducted at Hitler's birthday. His interrogator after the war is a tough, sceptical American officer. Major Steve Arnold challenges Furtwängler about why he stayed in Germany at all and he answers that he could not leave his country in her deepest misery. 'After all, I am a German. I – I stayed in my homeland. Is that my sin in your eyes?'[63]

In *Copenhagen* Heisenberg explains his patriotism to Bohr. 'Germany is where I was born,' he says. 'Germany is where I became what I am. Germany is all the faces of my childhood . . . Germany is my widowed mother and my impossible brother. Germany is my wife. Germany is our children' (p. 42). Heisenberg was not a Nazi sympathiser. He had been attacked as a 'white Jew' for his teaching of theoretical physics and had been interrogated by the SS. 'He was a rather romantically patriotic German,' Frayn explained in an interview, 'and that seems to me to be no less acceptable than to be a romantically patriotic Englishman or American. There are moral drawbacks in all those cases, and for Germans in the Nazi period to find any decent way to behave was very, very difficult.'[64]

Frayn discusses in the postscripts to *Copenhagen* the views of a number of scholars who take exception to his version of Heisenberg. Professor Paul Lawrence Rose has complained about 'subtle revisionism' in the 'denigration' of Bohr and the 'exalting' of Heisenberg (p. 133). Frayn's position is humane in that it acknowledges the extent of the predicament facing Germans during this period. 'I am astonished by the ease with which British and American commentators have condemned him,' Frayn said. 'People who were never called upon to make any great moral decisions in their life find it so easy to condemn Heisenberg for not taking a heroic stand. I think you can admire people who are heroes, but you can't *require* people to be heroes – otherwise there's no point in admiring them when they *are* heroic.'[65]

To approach *Copenhagen* as a play that asks us to give either the thumbs-up or the thumbs-down to Heisenberg is to miss many of the levels on which it operates. It does not deny the need for moral judgement. But Frayn's primary interest is in describing what happened. That has to come first. 'I am not making a case either for or against Heisenberg,' Frayn said. 'What I'm saying is that it is extremely difficult to know what his motivation was and this is an example of what applies to all human motivation – this difficulty of knowing why people do what they do.'[66]

This is, finally, the point where Frayn's professional interest in philosophy intersects with his lay interest in physics. In *Copenhagen* he shows that there is a theoretical barrier beyond which it is impossible to know precisely how a particle is behaving. You can only see it from one point of view at a time. In the same way we can only understand human actions from individual perspectives. Those who have disagreed with Frayn's portrayal of Heisenberg, for instance, do not agree with each other about how Heisenberg should be portrayed.

The best answer that the play gives, as to why Heisenberg made that trip to Copenhagen, was that he wanted to see his own reflection. 'We can understand many complex things,' Frayn had written twenty years before in *Constructions*, 'but not our own complexity!'[67] Heisenberg wanted to know what it was he was doing by talking it through with Bohr. But perhaps, in one final twist, he wouldn't really have wanted to find out what it was that he was doing. In one of the most important speeches of the play Margrethe says to Bohr:

> That was the last and greatest demand that Heisenberg made on his friendship with you. To be understood when he couldn't understand himself. And that was the last and greatest act of friendship for Heisenberg that you performed in return. To leave him misunderstood. (p. 89)

## The characters

The emotional currents between the three characters in *Copenhagen* give the play its questing energy. They are not debating a dry academic question. The characters have something to prove to one another. The central relationship in *Copenhagen* is the complex one between Bohr and Heisenberg, which resembles that of a father and son. As with many father–son relationships there is a shift in power. These two characters are well-contrasted. Heisenberg often led the way, working at great speed. Bohr followed, making sure the ideas worked. The contrast can be seen in the way

they skied. Heisenberg hurtled down slopes at breakneck
speed. Bohr went so slowly he nearly ground to a halt. In
the fable, one would be the tortoise, the other the hare.
Bohr's wife, Margrethe, injects a strong sense of conflict
into the trio. She supports her husband against his protégé.
Her presence ensures that these conflicts are made explicit.


*Werner Heisenberg (1901–76)*
German theoretical physicist. His childhood in Munich
ended with the outbreak of the First World War. As a
schoolboy Heisenberg had to crawl through enemy lines to
scavenge for food for his family. When he was twenty he
met Niels Bohr at Göttingen. Bohr was one of the most
celebrated physicists in the world. Heisenberg was the
'cheeky young pup' who jumped up at the end of a lecture
that Bohr had given and told Bohr that his mathematics
was wrong. That same afternoon Bohr and Heisenberg
went for the first of many walks. On the walk Bohr told
Heisenberg that *atoms were not things.* This news, Heisenberg
said, was the start of his real scientific career. Heisenberg
completed his doctorate when he was twenty-two and went
to join Bohr in Copenhagen. At this point Heisenberg was
shy, arrogant and anxious to be loved. After a year
Heisenberg had invented quantum mechanics. After another
year he had come up with the Principle of Uncertainty.
The year after that Heisenberg left Copenhagen to take up
the professorship at Leipzig. He was twenty-six – the
youngest full professor in Germany. In 1932 he was
awarded the Nobel Prize for Physics. Five years later he
met Elisabeth Schumacher, got engaged to her within two
weeks, and married her within three months. (They would
have seven children.) That same year Heisenberg was
viciously attacked in an SS magazine, which called him a
'white Jew' for teaching relativity. The SS interrogated him
in their basement headquarters at the Prinz-Albrecht-
Strasse. It took a year for his name to be cleared. He was

warned not to mention Einstein in his lectures. Before the
Second World War broke out Heisenberg turned down job
offers in America. During the war he was put in charge of
the German nuclear reactor programme.

In September 1941, when the meeting in *Copenhagen* takes
place, Heisenberg was nearly forty. The humble assistant
had become a middle-aged professor. He was the leading
scientist in a nation that had conquered most of Europe
('our tanks are almost at Moscow'). What Heisenberg had
to say to Bohr that night was treasonable and could have
led to his execution. Nine months later Heisenberg had a
meeting with Albert Speer, the Minister of Armaments, in
which he convinced Speer that an atom bomb could not be
produced before the end of the war. As the Allies' bombing
of German cities increased, Heisenberg witnessed terrible
scenes in Berlin, with people burning to death in the street.
He left Berlin, taking his scientific equipment south, to a
little village, Haigerloch, in the Swabian Jura. In the final
weeks of the war he managed to escape shooting as a
'deserter' by offering an SS officer a packet of cigarettes. In
April 1945 he was captured by the Allies and taken to
Farm Hall near Cambridge as a detainee. In early August,
while still a detainee, he heard on the BBC the news about
the atom bomb. After the war, Heisenberg faced thirty
years of reproach and hostility from scientists around the
world. He visited Bohr in Copenhagen in 1947. It became
clear that their friendship was over. Heisenberg revisited
America in 1949. Many physicists refused to shake his
hand.

Heisenberg was a patriot. He had wanted to save the
honour of German science. He never claimed to be a hero.
(At times, during the war, he showed considerable courage.)
He had a restless combative nature. He took little pleasure
in paradoxes and contradictions. He sailed, skied fast and
played the piano. (He could play chess without a
chessboard.) In *Celia's Secret* Frayn writes that Matthew
Marsh, who originated the role of Heisenberg, had

totally 'embodied the ambiguity and deviousness of Heisenberg'.[68]

*Niels Bohr (1885–1962)*
Denmark's leading theoretical physicist. He was half-Jewish. Bohr inspired love. He was a father-like figure to many younger physicists. (His pupils called him 'the Pope' behind his back.) Modern atomic physics began in 1913 when Bohr realised that quantum theory applied to matter as well as energy. He was thirty-eight when he started his three-year collaboration with the young Heisenberg. By 1941, when Heisenberg visited Bohr in Copenhagen, Denmark was occupied by Germany and Bohr was under surveillance. Bohr escaped from Denmark in 1943, crawling along the beach in the darkness on his hands and knees. A fishing boat took him across the Sound as two freighters arrived with orders to ship the Jewish population east. He had escaped the Holocaust. Bohr went to America and worked on the Allies' atomic bomb programme at Los Alamos. Specifically, he worked on the trigger for the Nagasaki bomb. 'My small but helpful part in the deaths of a hundred thousand people' (p. 91).

Bohr sailed, skied (slowly) and was highly competitive. Frayn shows his diplomatic manner ('Not to disagree, but', p. 25). But Bohr can also appear aggressive, as he prowls up and down demanding answers to questions. His sheer persistence had – at separate times – reduced Heisenberg and Bohr's wife, Margrethe, to tears. When the physicist Erwin Schrödinger came to stay Schrödinger had to retire to bed saying that he was ill. Bohr loved paradoxes and contradictions. He believed that science has to be expressed in plain language. Thomas Powers describes Bohr as 'searching, one painful word at a time, for some way to describe the essential strangeness of the subatomic world'.[69] Bohr defined an expert as someone who has made every conceivable mistake within a very narrow field. In *Celia's Secret* Frayn praised David Burke, the actor who originated the role of Bohr, for his incarnation of 'percipience and innocence, of toughness and lovability'.[70]

*Margrethe Bohr (1890–1984)*
Danish wife of Niels Bohr and his intimate companion. Margrethe never entirely liked Heisenberg. ('We had sons of our own' p.6.) Two of her six children died young. Christian, the firstborn, died in 1934 when he was out sailing with his father. The youngest, Harald, was incapacitated by a disease (thought by Bohr's biographer Abraham Pais to be meningitis), spent his life in institutions, and died aged about ten. Margrethe had no scientific training. Her knowledge, for instance, of complementarity came from typing out her husband's work again and again. In the play Margrethe thinks of herself as unfailingly courteous, unchangingly guarded. But she has a tendency to make everything personal. She is the audience's representative. Without her, the conversation would quickly become an exchange conducted in scientific shorthand between two experts. Margrethe also represents the many people who took a hostile view towards Heisenberg. In *Copenhagen* Margrethe is a severe, sceptical antagonist. She is outspoken in her criticisms. In real life, it must be said, she has been remembered as 'the perfect hostess'.[71]

## The play in production

When *Copenhagen* opened in 1998, it felt thoroughly modern in its concerns and presentation. The hackneyed images of World War Two dramas were absent. There were no Nazi uniforms, clicking heels, goosesteps, cod German accents or *Heil Hitler*s. Nor were there the clichés of wild-eyed scientists chalking up diagrams on blackboards. The designer, Peter J. Davison, had constructed a stage that was circular, white and clinical. Some members of the audience sat at the back of the stage. It suggested a laboratory or courtroom or – to those who were less admiring – a lecture hall. 'When the audience comes in,' said the director, Michael Blakemore, 'they see what is in front of them, and it's obvious that is what they [are going to] get: three actors, three chairs and a very good text. It makes them sit up and listen hard because there's nothing else.'[72]

The diagnostic atmosphere, free from any period trappings, was possible because the play is set in the future. Bohr died in 1962, Heisenberg died in 1976 and Margrethe died in 1984. *Copenhagen* brings them together in a kind of present day. The shifts in time between the 1920s, 1940s and this 'afterlife' might sound hard to follow on the printed page. Onstage it feels perfectly natural. Certainly Frayn didn't think he was devising a complicated or artificial convention: 'We do, all of us, live in different time zones. In the most ordinary way we are remembering things that happened yesterday and things that happened twenty years ago. We are worrying about things that might or might not happen tomorrow, or next year, and we switch back and forth from one to the other quite informally and effortlessly.'[73]

It was a liberating device. When theatre is stripped down, it can move as fast as the imagination. 'In order for theatre to maintain its vitality and its interest,' said Blakemore, 'it has to do something that the other, better-equipped mediums, can't do.'[74] The script of *Copenhagen* doesn't have a single stage direction. Blakemore's powerful production turned that into a strength. It was stark and focused. Only three metal chairs stood on a white circular floor on which the cast circled round and round. The easiest job on the production team had belonged to the props buyer. All that was required was Bohr's pipe. Even that wasn't essential. 'You could do without the pipe if you wanted,'[75] said Blakemore. There were a few sound effects: a train, a seagull, a doorbell, the rumble of the atomic bomb. Otherwise switches in lighting denoted shifts in time, place and points of view. There was none of the usual naturalistic clutter. The cast did not shuffle scientific papers, pour out drinks for one another or lay the table for dinner.

The changes in atmosphere came down to the expert nuances of the actors.

The three actors in the original production gave performances of transparent integrity. There was no showiness. The cast chased the ideas with an unrelenting vigour. David Burke's Bohr had a clubbable charm and a dose of irony. Matthew Marsh played Heisenberg with a furrowed earnestness and a rapid deadpan delivery. As Margrethe, Sara Kestelman had a caustic intelligence that saw events in refreshingly personal terms.

In its own elegant and elaborate way *Copenhagen* follows the traditional three-act structure. 'They go notionally through the meeting in Copenhagen three times,' Frayn said. 'First they say remembering something is like being there again, and they actually go through the meeting. Then at the end of the Act, Bohr says, "Let's try it again," and he arrives at the house a second time, and we then switch back to what it was like in the 1920s when they were doing theoretical research together. At the end of the play he agrees that they still haven't hit upon an explanation as to why he went to Copenhagen, and Bohr says, "Let's do one final draft." He arrives at the house and this time you just hear odd lines of that scene, while we hear the thoughts of the characters as they look at each other, and try to work out what the other is doing.'[76]

There was one aspect of *Copenhagen* that Blakemore thought that neither he nor Frayn had fully appreciated before the play opened. It was a very obvious point and it worked strongly in the play's favour. *Copenhagen* deals with 'an *extremely* important subject, namely atomic annihilation. The moment someone says "plutonium" in the play, everybody in the audience sits up and starts paying close attention.'[77]

## *Copenhagen* and the critics

*Copenhagen* opened at the Cottesloe Theatre, Royal National Theatre on 28 May 1998. When the reviews came out over the next few days it was clear that the critics were agreed on one point. None of them knew very much about physics. The *Financial Times* admitted: 'My physics ended way before O-level.' *The Times* admitted: 'Those of us whose physics stops short of changing lightbulbs . . .' The *Evening Standard* admitted: 'Those like me, without a shred of scientific knowledge . . .' The *Daily Mail* admitted: 'I absolutely switch off at any mention of matrix calculus or electrons passing through the cloud chamber.' The *Daily Telegraph* admitted: 'I got the lowest possible grade in chemistry-with-physics O-level.' The *Daily Express* admitted: 'Frankly, my brain started shorting out when we got on to nuclear fission.' The *Mail on Sunday*'s critic recorded the scene in the aisles before the play opened: 'The chatter in the audience before *Copenhagen* was whether physics O-level would be adequate for a two-and-a-half-hour discussion of quantum mechanics, uncertainty theory and the development of the atomic bomb. As it turned out, a degree in philosophy would have been more useful.'

Many of those who knew little about physics went on to admire the play. The *Financial Times* said it was 'a virtuoso exercise in dramatic irony'. *The Times* said 'it brims with intellectual excitement'. The *Daily Telegraph* said, 'Frayn makes ideas sing and zing.' The *Mail on Sunday* said it was 'brilliant, brave and demanding'. The *Guardian* said that *Copenhagen* is 'a logical extension of everything that he has done before'. 'It is unquestionably a play for non-scientists too,' said the *Independent on Sunday*. 'It deals with politics on the largest scale imaginable, and personal relationships at their most private and unspoken.' For the *Independent on Sunday* it was the best play of the year. *Copenhagen* went on to win the *Evening Standard* award for best new play.

The press reviews in the first week dealt with the play's success (or some thought, lack of it) as an evening in the theatre. Some regretted that there weren't more jokes. Some felt that the pared-down staging meant that it could have been a radio play. Some felt there was too much physics and it could have been a lecture. Except for an outburst by the poet and critic Tom Paulin on *Late*

*Review*, the reactions to the play, in terms of how accurately it represented the period, or the way it treated the scientific issues, took longer to emerge. As enthusiasm for the play grew so did the controversy about its portrayal of Heisenberg. This debate increased significantly when *Copenhagen* opened on Broadway. (In his Postscript Frayn deals with a number of the specific criticisms that have been made.)

*Copenhagen* received enough strong positive reviews to ensure a good audience. It soon became clear to the theatre-going public that here was an excellent production of an extremely intelligent play that dealt with one of the most important subjects of our time. There was always going to be an audience for that. Eight months after its opening *Copenhagen* transferred to the West End. Two years after its London première *Copenhagen* opened on Broadway. It won the 2000 Tony award for best play. Frayn had once written that plays could be classified in many ways, but the two most fundamental categories were 'hits' and 'flops'. *Copenhagen* was a hit.

[1] John Lanchester, *New York Review of Books*, 27 June 2002
[2] Claire Armistead, *Guardian*, 31 January 2002
[3] Duncan Wu (ed.), *Making Plays* (Macmillan, 2000), p.248
[4] www.bombsite.com/frayn
[5] P.M.S. Hacker, *Wittgenstein* (Phoenix, 2002), p.25
[6] Ibid., p.4
[7] 'The Battle of the Books' in *The Original Michael Frayn* (Methuen, 1990), p.130
[8] 'Creating Copenhagen', Dramatists Guild Website
[9] www.guardian.co.uk/saturday_review (14 August 1999)
[10] *The Two of Us* (Samuel French, 1970), p.33
[11] *The Russian Interpreter* (Penguin, 1967), p.51
[12] *Constructions* (Wildwood House, 1974), 160
[13] *Towards the End of the Morning* (Faber, 2000), pp.76–89
[14] *Constructions*, 185
[15] *Clouds* in *Frayn Plays: One* (Methuen, 1985), p.179
[16] Thomas Powers, *Heisenberg's War* (Cape, 1993), p.1

[17] www.bombsite.com/frayn
[18] *The Original Michael Frayn*, pp.213–16
[19] Ibid., p.197
[20] *Headlong* (Faber, 1999), p.25
[21] *The Original Michael Frayn*, p.196
[22] www.argument.independent.co.uk (17 May 2001)
[23] *Alphabetical Order* in *Frayn Plays: One*, p.39
[24] Ibid., p.8
[25] *Donkeys' Years* in *Frayn Plays: One*, p.52
[26] *Clouds* in *Frayn Plays: One*, p.239
[27] *Benefactors* in *Frayn Plays: Two*, p.14
[28] Ibid., p.58
[29] www.telegraph.co.uk (30 May 1998)
[30] *Headlong*, p.122
[31] Mark Arnold-Foster, *The World at War* (Pimlico, 2001), p.185
[32] Edward Davidson and Dale Manning, *Chronology of World War Two* (Cassell & Co., 1999), p.252
[33] David Halberstam, *The Fifties* (Fawcett Columbine, 1993), p.31
[34] Jeremy Bernstein (ed.), *Hitler's Uranium Club* (Copernicus Books, 2001), p.20
[35] R.A.C. Parker, *The Second World War: A Short History* (OUP, 2001), p.1
[36] *The Fifties*, pp.29 and 34
[37] *Off the Record: The Private Papers of Harry S. Truman*, 25 July 1945 (Harper & Row, 1986)
[38] *The Fifties*, p.24
[39] *Hitler's Uranium Club*, p.357
[40] *Heisenberg's War*, p.vii
[41] web.gc.cuny.edu/ashp/nml/Copenhagen/Cassidy.htm
[42] *Heisenberg's War*, p.122
[43] *Making Plays*, p.216
[44] *Heisenberg's War*, p.118
[45] *Making Plays*, p.217
[46] www.broadwayinboston.com
[47] *Making Plays*, p.217
[40] Anthony Gardner, *Independent*, 7 May 2001
[49] Alistair Owen (ed.), *Smoking in Bed* (Bloomsbury, 2001), p.68
[50] Ibid., p.81
[51] www.bombsite.com/frayn
[52] *Constructions*, 298

[53] www.pbs.org/hollywoodpresents/copenhagen
[54] Robert Butler, *Independent on Sunday*, 20 September 1998
[55] Ibid.
[56] web.gc.cuny.educ/ashp/nml/Copenhagen/Cassidy.htm
[57] Ian Kershaw, *Hitler: Hubris* (Penguin, 2001), p.480
[58] Michael Burleigh, *The Third Reich* (Macmillan, 2000), p.11
[59] David Edgar, 'Afterword', *Albert Speer* (Nick Hern Books, 2000), p.151
[60] C.P. Taylor, 'Author's Note', *Good* (Methuen, 1982)
[61] *Albert Speer*, p.134
[62] Ibid., p.147
[63] Ronald Harwood, *Taking Sides* (Faber, 2002), p.152
[64] *Making Plays*, p.224
[65] Ibid.
[66] www.bombsite.com/frayn
[67] *Constructions*, 62
[68] Michael Frayn and David Burke, *Celia's Secret: An Investigation* (Faber, 2000), p.54
[69] *Heisenberg's War*, p.46
[70] *Celia's Secret*, p.vi
[71] web.gc.cuny.educ/ashp/nml/Copenhagen/Lustig_Schwartz.htm
[72] www.broadwayinboston.com
[73] *Making Plays*, p.229
[74] Ibid., p.238
[75] Ibid., p.249
[76] Ibid., p.229
[77] Ibid., p.239

# Further Reading

## Works by Michael Frayn

*Plays*

*Frayn Plays: One* (Methuen, 1985) contains *Alphabetical Order,
Donkeys' Years, Clouds, Make and Break, Noises Off*

*Frayn Plays: Two* (Methuen, 1991) contains *Benefactors,
Balmoral, Wild Honey*

*Frayn Plays: Three* (Methuen, 2000) contains *Here, Now You
Know, La Belle Vivette*

The subject matter in the plays differs widely but similar
themes to *Copenhagen* can be found in, for instance, *Clouds,
Alphabetical Order, Benefactors, Here* and *Noises Off. Democracy*
(Methuen, 2003) deals with politics and espionage in post-
war Germany.

*Non-fiction*

Michael Frayn and David Burke, *Celia's Secret: An Investigation*
(Faber, 2000). The story of how one of the actors in the
original production hoaxed Frayn with papers purporting
to relate to historical events described in the play. It
shows the playwright confronting a central theme of his
writing (how we know what we know)

*The Original Michael Frayn* (Methuen, 1990), a collection of
Frayn's early journalism

*The Additional Michael Frayn* (Methuen, 2000), Frayn's later
journalism

*Constructions* (Wildwood House Ltd, 1974), his one work of
philosophy

## Works about Michael Frayn

Malcolm Page, *File on Frayn* (Methuen, 1994)

Duncan Wu (ed.), *Making Plays* (Macmillan, 2000) contains
penetrating interviews with Frayn and Michael
Blakemore about *Copenhagen*

## Background

Frayn provides a reading list on pp.130–2 that directly
relates to Bohr, Heisenberg and the Copenhagen
Interpretation. On a more general level, Michael Burleigh's
*The Third Reich* is an excellent introduction to Germany in
the thirties and the theoretical physicist Richard Feynman's
*Six Easy Pieces* (Penguin, 1998) is a lively and concise
introduction to atomic physics and quantum behaviour.

## Film

Howard Davies directed Francesca Annis as Margrethe,
Stephen Rea as Bohr and Daniel Craig as Heisenberg in a
film adaptation of *Copenhagen*. The website that accompanies
the film provides a detailed timeline and glossary of terms
(www.pbs.org/hollywoodpresents/copenhagen).

## Websites

Other online resources include Dr Tom Kerns' introduction
to epistemology and quantum physics,
www.students.washington.educ/tkerns, and Harry Lustig's
biographies of the persons referred to in *Copenhagen*,
www.northonline.sccd.ctc.edu/wokcs/Copenhagen.

# Copenhagen

*Copenhagen* was first previewed at the Cottesloe Theatre, Royal National Theatre, London, on 21 May 1998, and opened on 28 May 1998, with the following cast:

**Margrethe**       Sara Kestelman
**Bohr**            David Burke
**Heisenberg**      Matthew Marsh

*Directed by* Michael Blakemore
*Designed by* Peter J. Davison
*Lighting by* Mark Henderson
*Sound by* Simon Baker

This production moved to the Duchess Theatre, London, where it was presented by Michael Codron and Lee Dean, and opened on 5 February 1999.

It previewed at the Royale Theatre, New York, on 23 March 2000, and opened on 11 April 2000, with the following cast:

**Margrethe**       Blair Brown
**Bohr**            Philip Bosco
**Heisenberg**      Michael Cumpsty

*Directed by* Michael Blakemore
*Designed by* Peter J. Davison
*Lighting by* Mark Henderson and Michael Lincoln
*Sound by* Tony Meola

This revised edition of the text, including an extended version of the Postscript and a diagrammatic outline of the play's scientific and historical background, is published to coincide with the production in New York.

# Act One

**Margrethe**  But why?

**Bohr**  You're still thinking about it?

**Margrethe**  Why did he come to Copenhagen?

**Bohr**  Does it matter, my love, now we're all three of us dead and gone?

**Margrethe**  Some questions remain long after their owners have died. Lingering like ghosts. Looking for the answers they never found in life.

**Bohr**  Some questions have no answers to find.

**Margrethe**  Why did he come? What was he trying to tell you?

**Bohr**  He did explain later.

**Margrethe**  He explained over and over again. Each time he explained it became more obscure.

**Bohr**  It was probably very simple, when you come right down to it: he wanted to have a talk.

**Margrethe**  A talk? To the enemy? In the middle of a war?

**Bohr**  Margrethe, my love, we were scarcely the enemy.

**Margrethe**  It was 1941!

**Bohr**  Heisenberg was one of our oldest friends.

**Margrethe**  Heisenberg was German. We were Danes. We were under German occupation.

**Bohr**  It put us in a difficult position, certainly.

**Margrethe**  I've never seen you as angry with anyone as you were with Heisenberg that night.

**Bohr**  Not to disagree, but I believe I remained

remarkably calm.

**Margrethe**   I know when you're angry.

**Bohr**   It was as difficult for him as it was for us.

**Margrethe**   So why did he do it? Now no one can be hurt, now no one can be betrayed.

**Bohr**   I doubt if he ever really knew himself.

**Margrethe**   And he wasn't a friend. Not after that visit. That was the end of the famous friendship between Niels Bohr and Werner Heisenberg.

**Heisenberg**   Now we're all dead and gone, yes, and there are only two things the world remembers about me. One is the uncertainty principle, and the other is my mysterious visit to Niels Bohr in Copenhagen in 1941. Everyone understands uncertainty. Or thinks he does. No one understands my trip to Copenhagen. Time and time again I've explained it. To Bohr himself, and Margrethe. To interrogators and intelligence officers, to journalists and historians. The more I've explained, the deeper the uncertainty has become. Well, I shall be happy to make one more attempt. Now we're all dead and gone. Now no one can be hurt, now no one can be betrayed.

**Margrethe**   I never entirely liked him, you know. Perhaps I can say that to you now.

**Bohr**   Yes, you did. When he was first here in the twenties? Of course you did. On the beach at Tisvilde with us and the boys? He was one of the family.

**Margrethe**   Something alien about him, even then.

**Bohr**   So quick and eager.

**Margrethe**   Too quick. Too eager.

**Bohr**   Those bright watchful eyes.

**Margrethe**   Too bright. Too watchful.

**Bohr**   Well, he was a very great physicist. I never

changed my mind about that.

**Margrethe**  They were all good, all the people who came to Copenhagen to work with you. You had most of the great pioneers in atomic theory here at one time or another.

**Bohr**  And the more I look back on it, the more I think Heisenberg was the greatest of them all.

**Heisenberg**  So what was Bohr? He was the first of us all, the father of us all. Modern atomic physics began when Bohr realised that quantum theory applied to matter as well as to energy. 1913. Everything we did was based on that great insight of his.

**Bohr**  When you think that he first came here to work with me in 1924 . . .

**Heisenberg**  I'd only just finished my doctorate, and Bohr was the most famous atomic physicist in the world.

**Bohr**  . . . and in just over a year he'd invented quantum mechanics.

**Margrethe**  It came out of his work with you.

**Bohr**  Mostly out of what he'd been doing with Max Born and Pascual Jordan at Göttingen. Another year or so and he'd got uncertainty.

**Margrethe**  And you'd done complementarity.

**Bohr**  We argued them both out together.

**Heisenberg**  We did most of our best work together.

**Bohr**  Heisenberg usually led the way.

**Heisenberg**  Bohr made sense of it all.

**Bohr**  We operated like a business.

**Heisenberg**  Chairman and managing director.

**Margrethe**  Father and son.

**Heisenberg**  A family business.

**Margrethe**   Even though we had sons of our own.

**Bohr**   And we went on working together long after he ceased to be my assistant.

**Heisenberg**   Long after I'd left Copenhagen in 1927 and gone back to Germany. Long after I had a chair and a family of my own.

**Margrethe**   Then the Nazis came to power. . . .

**Bohr**   And it got more and more difficult. When the war broke out – impossible. Until that day in 1941.

**Margrethe**   When it finished forever.

**Bohr**   Yes, why did he do it?

**Heisenberg**   September, 1941. For years I had it down in my memory as October.

**Margrethe**   September. The end of September.

**Bohr**   A curious sort of diary memory is.

**Heisenberg**   You open the pages, and all the neat headings and tidy jottings dissolve around you.

**Bohr**   You step through the pages into the months and days themselves.

**Margrethe**   The past becomes the present inside your head.

**Heisenberg**   September, 1941, Copenhagen. . . . And at once – here I am, getting off the night train from Berlin with my colleague Carl von Weizsäcker. Two plain civilian suits and raincoats among all the field-grey Wehrmacht uniforms arriving with us, all the naval gold braid, all the well-tailored black of the SS. In my bag I have the text of the lecture I'm giving. In my head is another communication that has to be delivered. The lecture is on astrophysics. The text inside my head is a more difficult one.

**Bohr**   We obviously can't go to the lecture.

**Margrethe**  Not if he's giving it at the German Cultural Institute – it's a Nazi propaganda organisation.

**Bohr**  He must know what we feel about that.

**Heisenberg**  Weizsäcker has been my John the Baptist, and written to warn Bohr of my arrival.

**Margrethe**  He wants to see you?

**Bohr**  I assume that's why he's come.

**Heisenberg**  But how can the actual meeting with Bohr be arranged?

**Margrethe**  He must have something remarkably important to say.

**Heisenberg**  It has to seem natural. It has to be private.

**Margrethe**  You're not really thinking of inviting him to the house?

**Bohr**  That's obviously what he's hoping.

**Margrethe**  Niels! They've occupied our country!

**Bohr**  He is not they.

**Margrethe**  He's one of them.

**Heisenberg**  First of all there's an official visit to Bohr's workplace, the Institute for Theoretical Physics, with an awkward lunch in the old familiar canteen. No chance to talk to Bohr, of course. Is he even present? There's Rozental . . . Petersen, I think . . . Christian Møller, almost certainly. . . . It's like being in a dream. You can never quite focus the precise details of the scene around you. At the head of the table – is that Bohr? I turn to look, and it's Bohr, it's Rozental, it's Møller, it's whoever I appoint to be there. . . . A difficult occasion, though – I remember that clearly enough.

**Bohr**  It was a disaster. He made a very bad impression. Occupation of Denmark unfortunate. Occupation of Poland, however, perfectly acceptable. Germany now certain to win the war.

**Heisenberg**   Our tanks are almost at Moscow. What can stop us? Well, one thing, perhaps. One thing.

**Bohr**   He knows he's being watched, of course. One must remember that. He has to be careful about what he says.

**Margrethe**   Or he won't be allowed to travel abroad again.

**Bohr**   My love, the Gestapo planted microphones in his house. He told Goudsmit when he was in America. The SS brought him in for interrogation in the basement at the Prinz-Albrecht-Strasse.

**Margrethe**   And then they let him go again.

**Heisenberg**   I wonder if they suspect for one moment how painful it was to get permission for this trip. The humiliating appeals to the Party, the demeaning efforts to have strings pulled by our friends in the Foreign Office.

**Margrethe**   How did he seem? Is he greatly changed?

**Bohr**   A little older.

**Margrethe**   I still think of him as a boy.

**Bohr**   He's nearly forty. A middle-aged professor, fast catching up with the rest of us.

**Margrethe**   You still want to invite him here?

**Bohr**   Let's add up the arguments on either side in a reasonably scientific way. Firstly, Heisenberg is a friend. . . .

**Margrethe**   Firstly, Heisenberg is a German.

**Bohr**   A White Jew. That's what the Nazis called him. He taught relativity, and they said it was Jewish physics. He couldn't mention Einstein by name, but he stuck with relativity, in spite of the most terrible attacks.

**Margrethe**   All the real Jews have lost their jobs. He's still teaching.

**Bohr**  He's still teaching relativity.

**Margrethe**  Still a professor at Leipzig.

**Bohr**  At Leipzig, yes. Not at Munich. They kept him out of the chair at Munich.

**Margrethe**  He could have been at Columbia.

**Bohr**  Or Chicago. He had offers from both.

**Margrethe**  He wouldn't leave Germany.

**Bohr**  He wants to be there to rebuild German science when Hitler goes. He told Goudsmit.

**Margrethe**  And if he's being watched it will all be reported upon. Who he sees. What he says to them. What they say to him.

**Heisenberg**  I carry my surveillance around like an infectious disease. But then I happen to know that Bohr is also under surveillance.

**Margrethe**  And you know you're being watched yourself.

**Bohr**  By the Gestapo?

**Heisenberg**  Does he realise?

**Bohr**  I've nothing to hide.

**Margrethe**  By our fellow-Danes. It would be a terrible betrayal of all their trust in you if they thought you were collaborating.

**Bohr**  Inviting an old friend to dinner is hardly collaborating.

**Margrethe**  It might appear to be collaborating.

**Bohr**  Yes. He's put us in a difficult position.

**Margrethe**  I shall never forgive him.

**Bohr**  He must have good reason. He must have very good reason.

**Heisenberg**  This is going to be a deeply awkward occasion.

**Margrethe**   You won't talk about politics?

**Bohr**   We'll stick to physics. I assume it's physics he wants to talk to me about.

**Margrethe**   I think you must also assume that you and I aren't the only people who hear what's said in this house. If you want to speak privately you'd better go out in the open air.

**Bohr**   I shan't want to speak privately.

**Margrethe**   You could go for another of your walks together.

**Heisenberg**   Shall I be able to suggest a walk?

**Bohr**   I don't think we shall be going for any walks. Whatever he has to say he can say where everyone can hear it.

**Margrethe**   Some new idea he wants to try out on you, perhaps.

**Bohr**   What can it be, though? Where are we off to next?

**Margrethe**   So now of course your curiosity's aroused, in spite of everything.

**Heisenberg**   So now here I am, walking out through the autumn twilight to the Bohrs' house at Ny-Carlsberg. Followed, presumably, by my invisible shadow. What am I feeling? Fear, certainly – the touch of fear that one always feels for a teacher, for an employer, for a parent. Much worse fear about what I have to say. About how to express it. How to broach it in the first place. Worse fear still about what happens if I fail.

**Margrethe**   It's not something to do with the war?

**Bohr**   Heisenberg is a theoretical physicist. I don't think anyone has yet discovered a way you can use theoretical physics to kill people.

**Margrethe**   It couldn't be something about fission?

**Bohr**   Fission? Why would he want to talk to me about fission?

**Margrethe**   Because you're working on it.

**Bohr**   Heisenberg isn't.

**Margrethe**   Isn't he? Everybody else in the world seems to be. And you're the acknowledged authority.

**Bohr**   He hasn't published on fission.

**Margrethe**   It was Heisenberg who did all the original work on the physics of the nucleus. And he consulted you then, he consulted you at every step.

**Bohr**   That was back in 1932. Fission's only been around for the last three years.

**Margrethe**   But if the Germans were developing some kind of weapon based on nuclear fission . . .

**Bohr**   My love, no one is going to develop a weapon based on nuclear fission.

**Margrethe**   But if the Germans were trying to, Heisenberg would be involved.

**Bohr**   There's no shortage of good German physicists.

**Margrethe**   There's no shortage of good German physicists in America or Britain.

**Bohr**   The Jews have gone, obviously.

**Heisenberg**   Einstein, Wolfgang Pauli, Max Born . . . Otto Frisch, Lise Meitner. . . . We led the world in theoretical physics! Once.

**Margrethe**   So who is there still working in Germany?

**Bohr**   Sommerfeld, of course. Von Laue.

**Margrethe**   Old men.

**Bohr**   Wirtz. Harteck.

**Margrethe** Heisenberg is head and shoulders above all of them.

**Bohr** Otto Hahn – he's still there. He discovered fission, after all.

**Margrethe** Hahn's a chemist. I thought that what Hahn discovered . . .

**Bohr** . . . was that Enrico Fermi had discovered it in Rome four years earlier. Yes – he just didn't realise it was fission. It didn't occur to anyone that the uranium atom might have split, and turned into an atom of barium and an atom of krypton. Not until Hahn and Strassmann did the analysis, and detected the barium.

**Margrethe** Fermi's in Chicago.

**Bohr** His wife's Jewish.

**Margrethe** So Heisenberg would be in charge of the work?

**Bohr** Margrethe, there is no work! John Wheeler and I did it all in 1939. One of the implications of our paper is that there's no way in the foreseeable future in which fission can be used to produce any kind of weapon.

**Margrethe** Then why is everyone still working on it?

**Bohr** Because there's an element of magic in it. You fire a neutron at the nucleus of a uranium atom and it splits into two other elements. It's what the alchemists were trying to do – to turn one element into another.

**Margrethe** So why is he coming?

**Bohr** Now your curiosity's aroused.

**Margrethe** My forebodings.

**Heisenberg** I crunch over the familiar gravel to the Bohrs' front door, and tug at the familiar bell-pull. Fear, yes. And another sensation, that's become painfully familiar over the past year. A mixture of self-importance and sheer helpless absurdity – that of all the 2,000 million people in this world, I'm the one who's been charged with this impossible responsibility. . . . *The heavy door swings open.*

**Bohr**   My dear Heisenberg!

**Heisenberg**   My dear Bohr!

**Bohr**   Come in, come in . . .

**Margrethe**   And of course as soon as they catch sight of each other all their caution disappears. The old flames leap up from the ashes. If we can just negotiate all the treacherous little opening civilities . . .

**Heisenberg**   I'm so touched you felt able to ask me.

**Bohr**   We must try to go on behaving like human beings.

**Heisenberg**   I realise how awkward it is.

**Bohr**   We scarcely had a chance to do more than shake hands at lunch the other day.

**Heisenberg**   And Margrethe I haven't seen . . .

**Bohr**   Since you were here four years ago.

**Margrethe**   Niels is right. You look older.

**Heisenberg**   I had been hoping to see you both in 1938, at the congress in Warsaw . . .

**Bohr**   I believe you had some personal trouble.

**Heisenberg**   A little business in Berlin.

**Margrethe**   In the Prinz-Albrecht-Strasse?

**Heisenberg**   A slight misunderstanding.

**Bohr**   We heard, yes. I'm so sorry.

**Heisenberg**   These things happen. The question is now resolved. Happily resolved. We should all have met in Zürich . . .

**Bohr**   In September 1939.

**Heisenberg**   Only of course . . .

**Margrethe**   There was an unfortunate clash with the outbreak of war.

**Heisenberg**   Sadly.

**Bohr**   Sadly for us, certainly.

**Margrethe**   A lot more sadly still for many people.

**Heisenberg**   Yes. Indeed.

**Bohr**   Well, there it is.

**Heisenberg**   What can I say?

**Margrethe**   What can any of us say, in the present circumstances?

**Heisenberg**   No. And your sons?

**Margrethe**   Are well, thank you. Elisabeth? The children?

**Heisenberg**   Very well. They send their love, of course.

**Margrethe**   They so much wanted to see each other, in spite of everything! But now the moment has come they're so busy avoiding each other's eye that they can scarcely see each other at all.

**Heisenberg**   I wonder if you realise how much it means to me to be back here in Copenhagen. In this house. I have become rather isolated in these last few years.

**Bohr**   I can imagine.

**Margrethe**   Me he scarcely notices. I watch him discreetly from behind my expression of polite interest as he struggles on.

**Heisenberg**   Have things here been difficult?

**Bohr**   Difficult?

**Margrethe**   Of course. He has to ask. He has to get it out of the way.

**Bohr**   Difficult. . . . What can I say? We've not so far been treated to the gross abuses that have occurred elsewhere. The race laws have not been enforced.

**Margrethe**   Yet.

**Bohr**  A few months ago they started deporting Communists and other anti-German elements.

**Heisenberg**  But you personally . . . ?

**Bohr**  Have been left strictly alone.

**Heisenberg**  I've been anxious about you.

**Bohr**  Kind of you. No call for sleepless nights in Leipzig so far, though.

**Margrethe**  Another silence. He's done his duty. Now he can begin to steer the conversation round to pleasanter subjects.

**Heisenberg**  Are you still sailing?

**Bohr**  Sailing?

**Margrethe**  Not a good start.

**Bohr**  No, no sailing.

**Heisenberg**  The Sound is . . . ?

**Bohr**  Mined.

**Heisenberg**  Of course.

**Margrethe**  I assume he won't ask if Niels has been ski-ing.

**Heisenberg**  You've managed to get some ski-ing?

**Bohr**  Ski-ing? In Denmark?

**Heisenberg**  In Norway. You used to go to Norway.

**Bohr**  I did, yes.

**Heisenberg**  But since Norway is also . . . well . . .

**Bohr**  Also occupied? Yes, that might make it easier. In fact I suppose we could now holiday almost anywhere in Europe.

**Heisenberg**  I'm sorry. I hadn't thought of it quite in those terms.

**Bohr**  Perhaps I'm being a little oversensitive.

**Heisenberg**    Of course not. I should have thought.

**Margrethe**    He must almost be starting to wish he was back in the Prinz-Albrecht-Strasse.

**Heisenberg**    I don't suppose you feel you could ever come to Germany . . .

**Margrethe**    The boy's an idiot.

**Bohr**    My dear Heisenberg, it would be an easy mistake to make, to think that the citizens of a small nation, of a small nation overrun, wantonly and cruelly overrun, by its more powerful neighbour, don't have exactly the same feelings of national pride as their conquerors, exactly the same love of their country.

**Margrethe**    Niels, we agreed.

**Bohr**    To talk about physics, yes.

**Margrethe**    Not about politics.

**Bohr**    I'm sorry.

**Heisenberg**    No, no – I was simply going to say that I still have my old ski-hut at Bayrischzell. So if by any chance . . . at any time . . . for any reason . . .

**Bohr**    Perhaps Margrethe would be kind enough to sew a yellow star on my ski-jacket.

**Heisenberg**    Yes. Yes. Stupid of me.

**Margrethe**    Silence again. Those first brief sparks have disappeared, and the ashes have become very cold indeed. So now of course I'm starting to feel almost sorry for him. Sitting here all on his own in the midst of people who hate him, all on his own against the two of us. He looks younger again, like the boy who first came here in 1924. Younger than Christian would have been now. Shy and arrogant and anxious to be loved. Homesick and pleased to be away from home at last. And, yes, it's sad, because Niels loved him, he was a father to him.

**Heisenberg**    So . . . what are you working on?

**Margrethe**   And all he can do is press forward.

**Bohr**   Fission, mostly.

**Heisenberg**   I saw a couple of papers in the *Physical Review*. The velocity-range relations of fission fragments . . . ?

**Bohr**   And something about the interactions of nuclei with deuterons. And you?

**Heisenberg**   Various things.

**Margrethe**   Fission?

**Heisenberg**   I sometimes feel very envious of your cyclotron.

**Margrethe**   Why? Are you working on fission yourself?

**Heisenberg**   There are over thirty in the United States. Whereas in the whole of Germany . . . Well. . . . You still get to your country place, at any rate?

**Bohr**   We still go to Tisvilde, yes.

**Margrethe**   In the whole of Germany, you were going to say . . .

**Bohr**   . . . there is not one single cyclotron.

**Heisenberg**   So beautiful at this time of year. Tisvilde.

**Bohr**   You haven't come to borrow the cyclotron, have you? That's not why you've come to Copenhagen?

**Heisenberg**   That's not why I've come to Copenhagen.

**Bohr**   I'm sorry. We mustn't jump to conclusions.

**Heisenberg**   No, we must none of us jump to conclusions of any sort.

**Margrethe**   We must wait patiently to be told.

**Heisenberg**   It's not always easy to explain things to the world at large.

**Bohr**   I realise that we must always be conscious of the wider audience our words may have. But the lack of cyclotrons in Germany is surely not a military secret.

**Heisenberg**  I've no idea what's a secret and what isn't.

**Bohr**  No secret, either, about why there aren't any. You can't say it but I can. It's because the Nazis have systematically undermined theoretical physics. Why? Because so many people working in the field were Jews. And why were so many of them Jews? Because theoretical physics, the sort of physics done by Einstein, by Schrödinger and Pauli, by Born and Sommerfeld, by you and me, was always regarded in Germany as inferior to experimental physics, and the theoretical chairs and lectureships were the only ones that Jews could get.

**Margrethe**  Physics, yes? Physics.

**Bohr**  This is physics.

**Margrethe**  It's also politics.

**Heisenberg**  The two are sometimes painfully difficult to keep apart.

**Bohr**  So, you saw those two papers. I haven't seen anything by you recently.

**Heisenberg**  No.

**Bohr**  Not like you. Too much teaching?

**Heisenberg**  I'm not teaching. Not at the moment.

**Bohr**  My dear Heisenberg – they haven't pushed you out of your chair at Leipzig? That's not what you've come to tell us?

**Heisenberg**  No, I'm still at Leipzig. For part of each week.

**Bohr**  And for the rest of the week?

**Heisenberg**  Elsewhere. The problem is more work, not less.

**Bohr**  I see. Do I?

**Heisenberg**  Are you in touch with any of our friends in England? Born? Chadwick?

**Bohr**  Heisenberg, we're under German occupation. Germany's at war with Britain.

**Heisenberg**  I thought you might still have contacts of some sort. Or people in America? We're not at war with America.

**Margrethe**  Yet.

**Heisenberg**  You've heard nothing from Pauli, in Princeton? Goudsmit? Fermi?

**Bohr**  What do you want to know?

**Heisenberg**  I was simply curious . . . I was thinking about Robert Oppenheimer the other day. I had a great set-to with him in Chicago in 1939.

**Bohr**  About mesons.

**Heisenberg**  Is he still working on mesons?

**Bohr**  I'm quite out of touch.

**Margrethe**  The only foreign visitor we've had was from Germany. Your friend Weizsäcker was here in March.

**Heisenberg**  *My* friend? *Your* friend, too. I hope. You know he's come back to Copenhagen with me? He's very much hoping to see you again.

**Margrethe**  When he came here in March he brought the head of the German Cultural Institute with him.

**Heisenberg**  I'm sorry about that. He did it with the best of intentions. He may not have explained to you that the Institute is run by the Cultural Division of the Foreign Office. We have good friends in the foreign service. Particularly at the Embassy here.

**Bohr**  Of course. I knew his father when he was Ambassador in Copenhagen in the twenties.

**Heisenberg**  It hasn't changed so much since then, you

know, the German foreign service.

**Bohr**    It's a department of the Nazi government.

**Heisenberg**    Germany is more complex than it may
perhaps appear from the outside. The different organs of
state have quite different traditions, in spite of all attempts
at reform. Particularly the foreign service. Our people in
the Embassy here are quite old-fashioned in the way they
use their influence. They would certainly be trying to see
that distinguished local citizens were able to work
undisturbed.

**Bohr**    Are you telling me that I'm being protected by
your friends in the Embassy?

**Heisenberg**    What I'm saying, in case Weizsäcker failed
to make it clear, is that you would find congenial company
there. I know people would be very honoured if you felt
able to accept an occasional invitation.

**Bohr**    To cocktail parties at the Germany Embassy? To
coffee and cakes with the Nazi plenipotentiary?

**Heisenberg**    To lectures, perhaps. To discussion groups.
Social contacts of any sort could be helpful.

**Bohr**    I'm sure they could.

**Heisenberg**    Essential, perhaps, in certain circumstances.

**Bohr**    In what circumstances?

**Heisenberg**    I think we both know.

**Bohr**    Because I'm half-Jewish?

**Heisenberg**    We all at one time or another may need
the help of our friends.

**Bohr**    Is this why you've come to Copenhagen? To invite
me to watch the deportation of my fellow-Danes from a
grandstand seat in the windows of the German Embassy?

**Heisenberg**    Bohr, please! Please! What else can I do?
How else can I help? It's an impossibly difficult situation

for you, I understand that. It's also an impossibly difficult one for me.

**Bohr**    Yes. I'm sorry. I'm sure you also have the best of intentions.

**Heisenberg**    Forget what I said. Unless . . .

**Bohr**    Unless I need to remember it.

**Heisenberg**    In any case it's not why I've come.

**Margrethe**    Perhaps you should simply say what it is you want to say.

**Heisenberg**    What you and I often used to do in the old days was to take an evening stroll.

**Bohr**    Often. Yes. In the old days.

**Heisenberg**    You don't feel like a stroll this evening, for old times' sake?

**Bohr**    A little chilly tonight, perhaps, for strolling.

**Heisenberg**    This is so difficult. You remember where we first met?

**Bohr**    Of course. At Göttingen in 1922.

**Heisenberg**    At a lecture festival held in your honour.

**Bohr**    It was a high honour. I was very conscious of it.

**Heisenberg**    You were being honoured for two reasons. Firstly because you were a great physicist . . .

**Bohr**    Yes, yes.

**Heisenberg**    . . . and secondly because you were one of the very few people in Europe who were prepared to have dealings with Germany. The war had been over for four years, and we were still lepers. You held out your hand to us. You've always inspired love, you know that. Wherever you've been, wherever you've worked. Here in Denmark. In England, in America. But in Germany we worshipped you. Because you held out your hand to us.

**Bohr**   Germany's changed.

**Heisenberg**   Yes. Then we were down. And you could be generous.

**Margrethe**   And now you're up.

**Heisenberg**   And generosity's harder. But you held out your hand to us then, and we took it.

**Bohr**   Yes. . . . No! Not you. As a matter of fact. You bit it.

**Heisenberg**   Bit it?

**Bohr**   Bit my hand! You did! I held it out, in my most statesmanlike and reconciliatory way, and you gave it a very nasty nip.

**Heisenberg**   *I* did?

**Bohr**   The first time I ever set eyes on you. At one of those lectures I was giving in Göttingen.

**Heisenberg**   What are you talking about?

**Bohr**   You stood up and laid into me.

**Heisenberg**   Oh . . . I offered a few comments.

**Bohr**   Beautiful summer's day. The scent of roses drifting in from the gardens. Rows of eminent physicists and mathematicians, all nodding approval of my benevolence and wisdom. Suddenly, up jumps a cheeky young pup and tells me that my mathematics are wrong.

**Heisenberg**   They were wrong.

**Bohr**   How old were you?

**Heisenberg**   Twenty.

**Bohr**   Two years younger than the century.

**Heisenberg**   Not quite.

**Bohr**   December 5th, yes?

**Heisenberg**   1.93 years younger than the century.

**Bohr**   To be precise.

**Heisenberg**   No – to two places of decimals. To be *precise*, 1.928 ... 7 ... 6 ... 7 ... 1 ...

**Bohr**   I can always keep track of you, all the same. And the century.

**Margrethe**   And Niels has suddenly decided to love him again, in spite of everything. Why? What happened? Was it the recollection of that summer's day in Göttingen? Or everything? Or nothing at all? Whatever it was, by the time we've sat down to dinner the cold ashes have started into flame once again.

**Bohr**   You were always so combative! It was the same when we played table-tennis at Tisvilde. You looked as if you were trying to kill me.

**Heisenberg**   I wanted to win. Of course I wanted to win. *You* wanted to win.

**Bohr**   I wanted an agreeable game of table-tennis.

**Heisenberg**   You couldn't see the expression on your face.

**Bohr**   I could see the expression on yours.

**Heisenberg**   What about those games of poker in the ski-hut at Bayrischzell, then? You once cleaned us all out! You remember that? With a non-existent straight! We're all mathematicians – we're all counting the cards – we're 90 per cent certain he hasn't got anything. But on he goes, raising us, raising us. This insane confidence. Until our faith in mathematical probability begins to waver, and one by one we all throw in.

**Bohr**   I thought I *had* a straight! I misread the cards! I bluffed myself!

**Margrethe**   Poor Niels.

**Heisenberg**   Poor Niels? He won! He bankrupted us! You were insanely competitive! He got us all playing poker once with imaginary cards!

**Bohr**   You played chess with Weizsäcker on an imaginary board!

**Margrethe**   Who won?

**Bohr**   Need you ask? At Bayrischzell we'd ski down from the hut to get provisions, and he'd make even that into some kind of race! You remember? When we were there with Weizsäcker and someone? You got out a stop-watch.

**Heisenberg**   It took poor Weizsäcker eighteen minutes.

**Bohr**   You were down there in ten, of course.

**Heisenberg**   Eight.

**Bohr**   I don't recall how long I took.

**Heisenberg**   Forty-five minutes.

**Bohr**   Thank you.

**Margrethe**   Some rather swift ski-ing going on here, I think.

**Heisenberg**   Your ski-ing was like your science. What were you waiting for? Me and Weizsäcker to come back and suggest some slight change of emphasis?

**Bohr**   Probably.

**Heisenberg**   You were doing seventeen drafts of each slalom?

**Margrethe**   And without me there to type them out.

**Bohr**   At least I knew where I was. At the speed you were going you were up against the uncertainty relationship. If you knew where you were when you were down you didn't know how fast you'd got there. If you knew how fast you'd been going you didn't know you were down.

**Heisenberg**   I certainly didn't stop to think about it.

**Bohr**   Not to criticise, but that's what might be criticised with some of your science.

**Heisenberg**   I usually got there, all the same.

**Bohr**   You never cared what got destroyed on the way, though. As long as the mathematics worked out you were satisfied.

**Heisenberg**   If something works it works.

**Bohr**   But the question is always, What does the mathematics mean, in plain language? What are the philosophical implications?

**Heisenberg**   I always knew you'd be picking your way step by step down the slope behind me, digging all the capsized meanings and implications out of the snow.

**Margrethe**   The faster you ski the sooner you're across the cracks and crevasses.

**Heisenberg**   The faster you ski the better you think.

**Bohr**   Not to disagree, but that is most . . . most interesting.

**Heisenberg**   By which you mean it's nonsense. But it's not nonsense. Decisions make themselves when you're coming downhill at seventy kilometres an hour. Suddenly there's the edge of nothingness in front of you. Swerve left? Swerve right? Or think about it and die? In your head you swerve both ways . . .

**Margrethe**   Like that particle.

**Heisenberg**   What particle?

**Margrethe**   The one that you said goes through two different slits at the same time.

**Heisenberg**   Oh, in our old thought-experiment. Yes. Yes!

**Margrethe**   Or Schrödinger's wretched cat.

**Heisenberg**   That's alive and dead at the same time.

**Margrethe**   Poor beast.

**Bohr**   My love, it was an imaginary cat.

**Margrethe**   I know.

**Bohr**   Locked away with an imaginary phial of cyanide.

**Margrethe**   I know, I know.

**Heisenberg**   So the particle's here, the particle's there . . .

**Bohr**   The cat's alive, the cat's dead . . .

**Margrethe**   You've swerved left, you've swerved right . . .

**Heisenberg**   Until the experiment is over, this is the point, until the sealed chamber is opened, the abyss detoured; and it turns out that the particle has met itself again, the cat's dead . . .

**Margrethe**   And you're alive.

**Bohr**   Not so fast, Heisenberg . . .

**Heisenberg**   The swerve itself was the decision.

**Bohr**   Not so fast, not so fast!

**Heisenberg**   Isn't that how you shot Hendrik Casimir dead?

**Bohr**   Hendrik Casimir?

**Heisenberg**   When he was working here at the Institute.

**Bohr**   I never shot Hendrik Casimir.

**Heisenberg**   You told me you did.

**Bohr**   It was George Gamow. I shot George Gamow. *You* don't know – it was long after your time.

**Heisenberg**   Bohr, you shot Hendrik Casimir.

**Bohr**   Gamow, Gamow. Because he insisted that it was always quicker to act than to react. To make a decision to do something rather than respond to someone else's doing it.

**Heisenberg**   And for that you shot him?

**Bohr**   It was him! He went out and bought a pair of pistols! He puts one in his pocket, I put one in mine, and we get on with the day's work. Hours go by, and we're arguing ferociously about – I can't remember – our problems with the nitrogen nucleus, I expect – when suddenly Gamow reaches into his pocket . . .

**Heisenberg**   Cap-pistols.

**Bohr**   Cap-pistols, yes. Of course.

**Heisenberg**   Margrethe was looking a little worried.

**Margrethe**   No – a little surprised. At the turn of events.

**Bohr**   Now you remember how quick he was.

**Heisenberg**   Casimir?

**Bohr**   Gamow.

**Heisenberg**   Not as quick as me.

**Bohr**   Of course not. But compared with me.

**Heisenberg**   A fast neutron. However, or so you're going to tell me . . .

**Bohr**   However, yes, before his gun is even out of his pocket . . .

**Heisenberg**   You've drafted your reply.

**Margrethe**   I've typed it out.

**Heisenberg**   You've checked it with Klein.

**Margrethe**   I've retyped it.

**Heisenberg**   You've submitted it to Pauli in Hamburg.

**Margrethe**   I've retyped it again.

**Bohr**   Before his gun is even out of his pocket, mine is in my hand.

**Heisenberg**   And poor Casimir has been blasted out of existence.

**Bohr**   Except that it was Gamow.

**Heisenberg**   It was Casimir! He told me!

**Bohr**   Yes, well, one of the two.

**Heisenberg**   Both of them simultaneously alive and dead in our memories.

**Bohr**   Like a pair of Schrödinger cats. Where were we?

**Heisenberg**   Ski-ing. Or music. That's another thing that decides everything for you. I play the piano and the way seems to open in front of me – all I have to do is follow. That's how I had my one success with women. At a musical evening at the Bückings in Leipzig – we've assembled a piano trio. 1937, just when all my troubles with the . . . when my troubles are coming to a head. We're playing the Beethoven G major. We finish the scherzo, and I look up from the piano to see if the others are ready to start the final presto. And in that instant I catch a glimpse of a young woman sitting at the side of the room. Just the briefest glimpse, but of course at once I've carried her off to Bayrischzell, we're engaged, we're married, etc. – the usual hopeless romantic fantasies. Then off we go into the presto, and it's terrifyingly fast – so fast there's no time to be afraid. And suddenly everything in the world seems easy. We reach the end and I just carry on ski-ing. Get myself introduced to the young woman – see her home – and, yes, a week later I've carried her off to Bayrischzell – another week and we're engaged – three months and we're married. All on the sheer momentum of that presto!

**Bohr**   You were saying you felt isolated. But you do have a companion, after all.

**Heisenberg**   Music?

**Bohr**   Elisabeth!

**Heisenberg**   Oh. Yes. Though, what with the children,

and so on . . . I've always envied the way you and Margrethe manage to talk about everything. Your work. Your problems. Me, no doubt.

**Bohr**  I was formed by nature to be a mathematically curious entity: not one but half of two.

**Heisenberg**  Mathematics becomes very odd when you apply it to people. One plus one can add up to so many different sums . . .

**Margrethe**  Silence. What's he thinking about now? His life? Or ours?

**Bohr**  So many things we think about at the same time. Our lives and our physics.

**Margrethe**  All the things that come into our heads out of nowhere.

**Bohr**  Our private consolations. Our private agonies.

**Heisenberg**  Silence. And of course they're thinking about their children again.

**Margrethe**  The same bright things. The same dark things. Back and back they come.

**Heisenberg**  Their four children living, and their two children dead.

**Margrethe**  Harald. Lying alone in that ward.

**Bohr**  She's thinking about Christian and Harald.

**Heisenberg**  The two lost boys. Harald . . .

**Bohr**  All those years alone in that terrible ward.

**Heisenberg**  And Christian. The firstborn. The eldest son.

**Bohr**  And once again I see those same few moments that I see every day.

**Heisenberg**  Those short moments on the boat, when the tiller slams over in the heavy sea, and Christian is falling.

**Bohr**   If I hadn't let him take the helm . . .

**Heisenberg**   Those long moments in the water.

**Bohr**   Those endless moments in the water.

**Heisenberg**   When he's struggling towards the lifebuoy.

**Bohr**   So near to touching it.

**Margrethe**   I'm at Tisvilde. I look up from my work.
There's Niels in the doorway, silently watching me. He
turns his head away, and I know at once what's happened.

**Bohr**   So near, so near! So slight a thing!

**Heisenberg**   Again and again the tiller slams over. Again
and again . . .

**Margrethe**   Niels turns his head away . . .

**Bohr**   Christian reaches for the lifebuoy . . .

**Heisenberg**   But about some things even they never
speak.

**Bohr**   About some things even we only think.

**Margrethe**   Because there's nothing to be said.

**Bohr**   Well . . . perhaps we *should* be warm enough. You
suggested a stroll.

**Heisenberg**   In fact the weather is remarkably warm.

**Bohr**   We shan't be long.

**Heisenberg**   A week at most.

**Bohr**   What – our great hike through Zealand?

**Heisenberg**   We went to Elsinore. I often think about
what you said there.

**Bohr**   You don't mind, my love? Half-an-hour?

**Heisenberg**   An hour, perhaps. No, the whole
appearance of Elsinore, you said, was changed by our
knowing that Hamlet had lived there. Every dark corner

there reminds us of the darkness inside the human soul . . .

**Margrethe**   So, they're walking again. He's done it. And if they're walking they're talking. Talking in a rather different way, no doubt – I've typed out so much in my time about how differently particles behave when they're unobserved . . . I knew Niels would never hold out if they could just get through the first few minutes. If only out of curiosity. . . . Now they're started an hour will mean two, of course, perhaps three. . . . The first thing they ever did was to go for a walk together. At Göttingen, after that lecture. Niels immediately went to look for the presumptuous young man who'd queried his mathematics, and swept him off for a tramp in the country. Walk – talk – make his acquaintance. And when Heisenberg arrived here to work for him, off they go again, on their great tour of Zealand. A lot of this century's physics they did in the open air. Strolling around the forest paths at Tisvilde. Going down to the beach with the children. Heisenberg holding Christian's hand. Yes, and every evening in Copenhagen, after dinner, they'd walk round Faelled Park behind the Institute, or out along Langelinie into the harbour. Walk, and talk. Long, long before walls had ears . . . But this time, in 1941, their walk takes a different course. Ten minutes after they set out . . . they're back! I've scarcely had the table cleared when there's Niels in the doorway. I see at once how upset he is – he can't look me in the eye.

**Bohr**   Heisenberg wants to say goodbye. He's leaving.

**Margrethe**   *He* won't look at me, either.

**Heisenberg**   Thank you. A delightful evening. Almost like old times. So kind of you.

**Margrethe**   You'll have some coffee? A glass of something?

**Heisenberg**   I have to get back and prepare for my lecture.

**Margrethe**   But you'll come and see us again before you leave?

**Bohr**   He has a great deal to do.

**Margrethe**   It's like the worst moments of 1927 all over again, when Niels came back from Norway and first read Heisenberg's uncertainty paper. Something they both seemed to have forgotten about earlier in the evening, though I hadn't. Perhaps they've both suddenly remembered that time. Only from the look on their faces something even worse has happened.

**Heisenberg**   Forgive me if I've done or said anything that . . .

**Bohr**   Yes, yes.

**Heisenberg**   It meant a great deal to me, being here with you both again. More perhaps than you realise.

**Margrethe**   It was a pleasure for us. Our love to Elisabeth.

**Bohr**   Of course.

**Margrethe**   And the children.

**Heisenberg**   Perhaps, when this war is over. . . . If we're all spared. . . . Goodbye.

**Margrethe**   Politics?

**Bohr**   Physics. He's not right, though. How can he be right? John Wheeler and I . . .

**Margrethe**   A breath of air as we talk, why not?

**Bohr**   A breath of air?

**Margrethe**   A turn around the garden. Healthier than staying indoors, perhaps.

**Bohr**   Oh. Yes.

**Margrethe**   For everyone concerned.

**Bohr**   Yes. Thank you. . . . How can he possibly be right? Wheeler and I went through the whole thing in 1939.

**Margrethe**   What did he say?

**Bohr**    Nothing. I don't know. I was too angry to take it in.

**Margrethe**    Something about fission?

**Bohr**    What happens in fission? You fire a neutron at a uranium nucleus, it splits, and it releases energy.

**Margrethe**    A huge amount of energy. Yes?

**Bohr**    About enough to move a speck of dust. But it also releases two or three more neutrons. Each of which has the chance of splitting another nucleus.

**Margrethe**    So then those two or three split nuclei each release energy in their turn?

**Bohr**    And two or three more neutrons.

**Heisenberg**    You start a trickle of snow sliding as you ski. The trickle becomes a snowball . . .

**Bohr**    An ever-widening chain of split nuclei forks through the uranium, doubling and quadrupling in millionths of a second from one generation to the next. First two splits, let's say for simplicity. Then two squared, two cubed, two to the fourth, two to the fifth, two to the sixth . . .

**Heisenberg**    The thunder of the gathering avalanche echoes from all the surrounding mountains . . .

**Bohr**    Until eventually, after, let's say, eighty generations, $2^{80}$ specks of dust have been moved. $2^{80}$ is a number with 24 noughts. Enough specks of dust to constitute a city, and all who live in it.

**Heisenberg**    But there is a catch.

**Bohr**    There is a catch, thank God. Natural uranium consists of two different isotopes. Most of it's U-238, which you can only fission with fast neutrons. Most neutrons, though, will only fission the other isotope, U-235 – and less than one per cent of natural uranium is U-235.

**Heisenberg**　This was Bohr's great insight. Another of his amazing intuitions. It came to him when he was at Princeton in 1939, walking across the campus with Wheeler. A characteristic Bohr moment – I wish I'd been there to enjoy it. Five minutes deep silence as they walked, then: 'Now hear this – I have understood everything.'

**Bohr**　In fact it's a double catch, because the 238 also slows neutrons down and absorbs them. So an explosive chain reaction will never occur in natural uranium. To make an explosion you will have to separate out pure 235. And to make the chain long enough for a large explosion . . .

**Heisenberg**　Eighty generations, let's say . . .

**Bohr**　. . . you would need many tons of it. And it's extremely difficult to separate.

**Heisenberg**　Tantalisingly difficult.

**Bohr**　Mercifully difficult. The best estimates, when I was in America in 1939, were that to produce even one gram of U-235 would take 26,000 years. By which time, surely, this war will be over. So he's wrong, you see, he's wrong! Or could *I* be wrong? Could I have miscalculated? Let me see. . . . What are the absorption rates for fast neutrons in 238? What's the mean free path of slow neutrons in 235 . . . ?

**Margrethe**　But what exactly had Heisenberg said? That's what everyone wanted to know, then and forever after.

**Bohr**　It's what the British wanted to know, as soon as Chadwick managed to get in touch with me. What exactly did Heisenberg say?

**Heisenberg**　And what exactly did Bohr reply? That was of course the first thing my colleagues asked me when I got back to Germany.

**Margrethe**　What did Heisenberg tell Niels – what did

Niels reply? The person who wanted to know most of all
was Heisenberg himself.

**Bohr**  You mean when he came back to Copenhagen
after the war, in 1947?

**Margrethe**  Escorted this time not by unseen agents of
the Gestapo, but by a very conspicuous minder from British
intelligence.

**Bohr**  I think he wanted various things.

**Margrethe**  Two things. Food-parcels . . .

**Bohr**  For his family in Germany. They were on the
verge of starvation.

**Margrethe**  And for you to agree what you'd said to
each other in 1941.

**Bohr**  The conversation went wrong almost as fast as it
did before.

**Margrethe**  You couldn't even agree where you'd walked
that night.

**Heisenberg**  Where we walked? Faelled Park, of course.
Where we went so often in the old days.

**Margrethe**  But Faelled Park is behind the Institute, four
kilometres away from where we live!

**Heisenberg**  I can see the drift of autumn leaves under
the street-lamps next to the bandstand.

**Bohr**  Yes, because you remember it as October!

**Margrethe**  And it was September.

**Bohr**  No fallen leaves!

**Margrethe**  And it was 1941. No street-lamps!

**Bohr**  I thought we hadn't got any further than my study.

What I can see is the drift of papers under the reading-lamp on my desk.

**Heisenberg**   We must have been outside! What I was going to say was treasonable. If I'd been overheard I'd have been executed.

**Margrethe**   So what was this mysterious thing you said?

**Heisenberg**   There's no mystery about it. There never was any mystery. I remember it absolutely clearly, because my life was at stake, and I chose my words very carefully. I simply asked you if as a physicist one had the moral right to work on the practical exploitation of atomic energy. Yes?

**Bohr**   I don't recall.

**Heisenberg**   You don't recall, no, because you immediately became alarmed. You stopped dead in your tracks.

**Bohr**   I was horrified.

**Heisenberg**   Horrified. Good, you remember that. You stood there gazing at me, horrified.

**Bohr**   Because the implication was obvious. That you *were* working on it.

**Heisenberg**   And you jumped to the conclusion that I was trying to provide Hitler with nuclear weapons.

**Bohr**   And you were!

**Heisenberg**   No! A reactor! That's what we were trying to build! A machine to produce power! To generate electricity, to drive ships!

**Bohr**   You didn't say anything about a reactor.

**Heisenberg**   I didn't say anything about anything! Not in so many words. I couldn't! I'd no idea how much could be overheard. How much you'd repeat to others.

**Bohr**   But then I asked you if you actually thought that uranium fission could be used for the construction of weapons.

**Heisenberg**  Ah! It's coming back!

**Bohr**  And I clearly remember what you replied.

**Heisenberg**  I said I now knew that it could be.

**Bohr**  This is what really horrified me.

**Heisenberg**  Because you'd always been confident that weapons would need 235, and that we could never separate enough of it.

**Bohr**  A reactor – yes, maybe, because you can keep a slow chain reaction going in natural uranium.

**Heisenberg**  What we'd realised, though, was that if we could once get the reactor going . . .

**Bohr**  The 238 in the natural uranium would absorb the fast neutrons . . .

**Heisenberg**  Exactly as you predicted in 1939 – everything we were doing was based on that fundamental insight of yours. The 238 would absorb the fast neutrons. And would be transformed by them into a new element altogether.

**Bohr**  Neptunium. Which would decay in its turn into another new element . . .

**Heisenberg**  At least as fissile as the 235 that we couldn't separate . . .

**Margrethe**  Plutonium.

**Heisenberg**  Plutonium.

**Bohr**  I should have worked it out for myself.

**Heisenberg**  If we could build a reactor we could build bombs. That's what had brought me to Copenhagen. But none of this could I say. And at this point you stopped listening. The bomb had already gone off inside your head. I realised we were heading back towards the house. Our walk was over. Our one chance to talk had gone forever.

**Bohr**   Because I'd grasped the central point already. That one way or another you saw the possibility of supplying Hitler with nuclear weapons.

**Heisenberg**   You grasped at least four different central points, all of them wrong. You told Rozental that I'd tried to pick your brains about fission. You told Weisskopf that I'd asked you what you knew about the Allied nuclear programme. Chadwick thought I was hoping to persuade you that there was no German programme. But then you seem to have told some people that I'd tried to recruit you to work on it!

**Bohr**   Very well. Let's start all over again from the beginning. No Gestapo in the shadows this time. No British intelligence officer. No one watching us at all.

**Margrethe**   Only me.

**Bohr**   Only Margrethe. We're going to make the whole thing clear to Margrethe. You know how strongly I believe that we don't do science for ourselves, that we do it so we can explain to others . . .

**Heisenberg**   In plain language.

**Bohr**   In plain language. Not your view, I know – you'd be happy to describe what you were up to purely in differential equations if you could – but for Margrethe's sake . . .

**Heisenberg**   Plain language.

**Bohr**   Plain language. All right, so here we are, walking along the street once more. And this time I'm absolutely calm, I'm listening intently. What is it you want to say?

**Heisenberg**   It's not just what *I* want to say! The whole German nuclear team in Berlin! Not Diebner, of course, not the Nazis – but Weizsäcker, Hahn, Wirtz, Jensen, Houtermanns – they all wanted me to come and discuss it with you. We all see you as a kind of spiritual father.

**Margrethe**   The Pope. That's what you used to call Niels behind his back. And now you want him to give you absolution.

**Heisenberg**   Absolution? No!

**Margrethe**   According to your colleague Jensen.

**Heisenberg**   Absolution is the last thing I want!

**Margrethe**   You told one historian that Jensen had expressed it perfectly.

**Heisenberg**   Did I? Absolution. . . . Is that what I've come for? It's like trying to remember who was at that lunch you gave me at the Institute. Around the table sit all the different explanations for everything I did. I turn to look . . . Petersen, Rozental, and . . . yes . . . now the word absolution is taking its place among them all . . .

**Margrethe**   Though I thought absolution was granted for sins past and repented, not for sins intended and yet to be committed.

**Heisenberg**   Exactly! That's why I was so shocked!

**Bohr**   *You* were shocked?

**Heisenberg**   Because you *did* give me absolution! That's exactly what you did! As we were hurrying back to the house. You muttered something about everyone in wartime being obliged to do his best for his own country. Yes?

**Bohr**   Heaven knows what I said. But now here I am, profoundly calm and conscious, weighing my words. You don't want absolution. I understand. You want me to tell you *not* to do it? All right. I put my hand on your arm. I look you in the eye in my most papal way. Go back to Germany, Heisenberg. Gather your colleagues together in the laboratory. Get up on a table and tell them: 'Niels Bohr says that in his considered judgment supplying a homicidal maniac with an improved instrument of mass murder is . . .' What shall I say? '. . . an interesting idea.' No, not even an interesting idea. '. . . a really rather seriously uninteresting idea.' What happens? You all fling down your Geiger counters?

**Heisenberg**  Obviously not.

**Bohr**  Because they'll arrest you.

**Heisenberg**  Whether they arrest us or not it won't make any difference. In fact it will make things worse. I'm running my programme for the Kaiser Wilhelm Institute. But there's a rival one at Army Ordnance, run by Kurt Diebner, and he's a party member. If I go they'll simply get Diebner to take over my programme as well. He should be running it anyway. Wirtz and the rest of them only smuggled me in to keep Diebner and the Nazis out of it. My one hope is to remain in control.

**Bohr**  So you don't want me to say yes and you don't want me to say no.

**Heisenberg**  What I want is for you to listen carefully to what I'm going on to say next, instead of running off down the street like a madman.

**Bohr**  Very well. Here I am, walking very slowly and popishly. And I listen most carefully as you tell me . . .

**Heisenberg**  That nuclear weapons will require an enormous technical effort.

**Bohr**  True.

**Heisenberg**  That they will suck up huge resources.

**Bohr**  Huge resources. Certainly.

**Heisenberg**  That sooner or later governments will have to turn to scientists and ask whether it's worth committing those resources – whether there's any hope of producing the weapons in time for them to be used.

**Bohr**  Of course, but . . .

**Heisenberg**  Wait. So they will have to come to you and me. We are the ones who will have to advise them whether to go ahead or not. In the end the decision will be in our hands, whether we like it or not.

**Bohr**   And that's what you want to tell me?

**Heisenberg**   That's what I want to tell you.

**Bohr**   That's why you have come all this way, with so much difficulty? That's why you have thrown away nearly twenty years of friendship? Simply to tell me that?

**Heisenberg**   Simply to tell you that.

**Bohr**   But, Heisenberg, this is more mysterious than ever! What are you telling it me *for*? What am I supposed to do about it? The government of occupied Denmark isn't going to come to me and ask me whether we should produce nuclear weapons!

**Heisenberg**   No, but sooner or later, if I manage to remain in control of our programme, the German government is going to come to *me*! They will ask *me* whether to continue or not! *I* will have to decide what to tell them!

**Bohr**   Then you have an easy way out of your difficulties. You tell them the simple truth that you've just told me. You tell them how difficult it will be. And perhaps they'll be discouraged. Perhaps they'll lose interest.

**Heisenberg**   But, Bohr, where will that lead? What will be the consequences if we manage to fail?

**Bohr**   What can I possibly tell you that you can't tell yourself?

**Heisenberg**   There was a report in a Stockholm paper that the Americans are working on an atomic bomb.

**Bohr**   Ah. Now it comes, now it comes. Now I understand everything. You think I have contacts with the Americans?

**Heisenberg**   You may. It's just conceivable. If anyone in Occupied Europe does it will be you.

**Bohr**   So you *do* want to know about the Allied nuclear programme.

**Heisenberg**   I simply want to know if there is one. Some hint. Some clue. I've just betrayed my country and risked my life to warn you of the German programme . . .

**Bohr**   And now I'm to return the compliment?

**Heisenberg**   Bohr, I have to know! I'm the one who has to decide! If the Allies are building a bomb, what am I choosing for my country? You said it would be easy to imagine that one might have less love for one's country if it's small and defenceless. Yes, and it would be another easy mistake to make, to think that one loved one's country less because it happened to be in the wrong. Germany is where I was born. Germany is where I became what I am. Germany is all the faces of my childhood, all the hands that picked me up when I fell, all the voices that encouraged me and set me on my way, all the hearts that speak to my heart. Germany is my widowed mother and my impossible brother. Germany is my wife. Germany is our children. I have to know what I'm deciding for them! Is it another defeat? Another nightmare like the nightmare I grew up with? Bohr, my childhood in Munich came to an end in anarchy and civil war. Are more children going to starve, as we did? Are they going to have to spend winter nights as I did when I was a schoolboy, crawling on my hands and knees through the enemy lines, creeping out into the country under cover of darkness in the snow to find food for my family? Are they going to sit up all night, as I did at the age of seventeen, guarding some terrified prisoner, talking to him and talking to him through the small hours, because he's going to be executed in the morning?

**Bohr**   But, my dear Heisenberg, there's nothing I can tell you. I've no idea whether there's an Allied nuclear programme.

**Heisenberg**   It's just getting under way even as you and I are talking. And maybe I'm choosing something worse even than defeat. Because the bomb they're building is to be used on us. On the evening of Hiroshima Oppenheimer said it was his one regret. That they hadn't produced the bomb in time to use on Germany.

**Bohr**   He tormented himself afterwards.

**Heisenberg**   Afterwards, yes. At least we tormented ourselves a little beforehand. Did a single one of them stop to think, even for one brief moment, about what they were doing? Did Oppenheimer? Did Fermi, or Teller, or Szilard? Did Einstein, when he wrote to Roosevelt in 1939 and urged him to finance research on the bomb? Did you, when you escaped from Copenhagen two years later, and went to Los Alamos?

**Bohr**   My dear, good Heisenberg, we weren't supplying the bomb to Hitler!

**Heisenberg**   You weren't dropping it on Hitler, either. You were dropping it on anyone who was in reach. On old men and women in the street, on mothers and their children. And if you'd produced it in time they would have been my fellow-countrymen. My wife. My children. That was the intention. Yes?

**Bohr**   That was the intention.

**Heisenberg**   You never had the slightest conception of what happens when bombs are dropped on cities. Even conventional bombs. None of you ever experienced it. Not a single one of you. I walked back from the centre of Berlin to the suburbs one night, after one of the big raids. No transport moving, of course. The whole city on fire. Even the puddles in the streets are burning. They're puddles of molten phosphorus. It gets on your shoes like some kind of incandescent dog-muck – I have to keep scraping it off – as if the streets have been fouled by the hounds of hell. It would have made you laugh – my shoes keep bursting into flame. All around me, I suppose, there are people trapped, people in various stages of burning to death. And all I can think is, How will I ever get hold of another pair of shoes in times like these?

**Bohr**   You know why Allied scientists worked on the bomb.

**Heisenberg**   Of course. Fear.

**Bohr**   The same fear that was consuming you. Because they were afraid that *you* were working on it.

**Heisenberg**   But, Bohr, you could have told them!

**Bohr**   Told them what?

**Heisenberg**   What I told you in 1941! That the choice is in our hands! In mine – in Oppenheimer's! That if I can tell them the simple truth when they ask me, the simple discouraging truth, so can he!

**Bohr**   This is what you want from me? Not to tell you what the Americans are doing but to stop them?

**Heisenberg**   To tell them that we can stop it together.

**Bohr**   I had no contact with the Americans!

**Heisenberg**   You did with the British.

**Bohr**   Only later.

**Heisenberg**   The Gestapo intercepted the message you sent them about our meeting.

**Margrethe**   And passed it to you?

**Heisenberg**   Why not? They'd begun to trust me. This is what gave me the possibility of remaining in control of events.

**Bohr**   Not to criticise, Heisenberg, but if this is your plan in coming to Copenhagen, it's ... what can I say? It's most interesting.

**Heisenberg**   It's not a plan. It's a hope. Not even a hope. A microscopically fine thread of possibility. A wild improbability. Worth trying, though, Bohr! Worth trying, surely! But already you're too angry to understand what I'm saying.

**Margrethe**   No – why he's angry is because he *is*
beginning to understand! The Germans drive out most of
their best physicists because they're Jews. America and
Britain give them sanctuary. Now it turns out that this
might offer the Allies a hope of salvation. And at once you
come howling to Niels begging him to persuade them to
give it up.

**Bohr**   Margrethe, my love, perhaps we should try to
express ourselves a little more temperately.

**Margrethe**   But the gall of it! The sheer, breathtaking
gall of it!

**Bohr**   Bold ski-ing, I have to say.

**Heisenberg**   But, Bohr, we're not ski-ing now! We're not
playing table-tennis! We're not juggling with cap-pistols and
non-existent cards! I refused to believe it, when I first heard
the news of Hiroshima. I thought that it was just one of
the strange dreams we were living in at the time. They'd
got stranger and stranger, God knows, as Germany fell into
ruins in those last months of the war. But by then we were
living in the strangest of them all. The ruins had suddenly
vanished – just the way things do in dreams – and all at
once we're in a stately home in the middle of the English
countryside. We've been rounded up by the British – the
whole team, everyone who worked on atomic research –
and we've been spirited away. To Farm Hall, in
Huntingdonshire, in the water-meadows of the River Ouse.
Our families in Germany are starving, and there are we
sitting down each evening to an excellent formal dinner
with our charming host, the British officer in charge of us.
It's like a pre-war house-party – one of those house-parties
in a play, that's cut off from any contact with the outside
world, where you know the guests have all been invited for
some secret sinister purpose. No one knows we're there –
no one in England, no one in Germany, not even our
families. But the war's over. What's happening? Perhaps, as
in a play, we're going to be quietly murdered, one by one.
In the meanwhile it's all delightfully civilised. I entertain the

party with Beethoven piano sonatas. Major Rittner, our
hospitable gaoler, reads Dickens to us, to improve our
English. . . . Did these things really happen to me . . . ? We
wait for the point of it all to be revealed to us. Then one
evening it is. And it's even more grotesque than the one we
were fearing. It's on the radio: you have actually done the
deed that we were tormenting ourselves about. That's why
we're there, dining with our gracious host, listening to our
Dickens. We've been kept locked up to stop us discussing
the subject with anyone until it's too late. When Major
Rittner tells us I simply refuse to believe it until I hear it
with my own ears on the nine o'clock news. We'd no idea
how far ahead you'd got. I can't describe the effect it has
on us. You play happily with your toy cap-pistol. Then
someone else picks it up and pulls the trigger . . . and all at
once there's blood everywhere and people screaming,
because it wasn't a toy at all. . . . We sit up half the night,
talking about it, trying to take it in. We're all literally in
shock.

**Margrethe**   Because it had been done? Or because it
wasn't you who'd done it?

**Heisenberg**   Both. Both. Otto Hahn wants to kill himself,
because it was he who discovered fission, and he can see
the blood on his hands. Gerlach, our old Government
administrator, also wants to die, because his hands are so
shamefully clean. You've done it, though. You've built the
bomb.

**Bohr**   Yes.

**Heisenberg**   And you've used it on a living target.

**Bohr**   On a living target.

**Margrethe**   You're not suggesting that Niels did anything
wrong in working at Los Alamos?

**Heisenberg**   Of course not. Bohr has never done
anything wrong.

**Margrethe**   The decision had been taken long before
Niels arrived. The bomb would have been built whether

Niels had gone or not.

**Bohr**    In any case, my part was very small.

**Heisenberg**    Oppenheimer described you as the team's father-confessor.

**Bohr**    It seems to be my role in life.

**Heisenberg**    He said you made a great contribution.

**Bohr**    Spiritual, possibly. Not practical.

**Heisenberg**    Fermi says it was you who worked out how to trigger the Nagasaki bomb.

**Bohr**    I put forward an idea.

**Margrethe**    You're not implying that there's anything that *Niels* needs to explain or defend?

**Heisenberg**    No one has ever expected him to explain or defend anything. He's a profoundly good man.

**Bohr**    It's not a question of goodness. I was spared the decision.

**Heisenberg**    Yes, and I was not. So explaining and defending myself was how I spent the last thirty years of my life. When I went to America in 1949 a lot of physicists wouldn't even shake my hand. Hands that had actually built the bomb wouldn't touch mine.

**Margrethe**    And let me tell you, if you think you're making it any clearer to me now, you're not.

**Bohr**    Margrethe, I understand his feelings ... .

**Margrethe**    I don't. I'm as angry as you were before! It's so easy to make you feel conscience-stricken. Why should he transfer his burden to you? Because what does he do after his great consultation with you? He goes back to Berlin and tells the Nazis that he can produce atomic bombs!

**Heisenberg**    But what I stress is the difficulty of separating 235.

**Margrethe**   You tell them about plutonium.

**Heisenberg**   I tell some of the minor officials. I have to keep people's hopes alive!

**Margrethe**   Otherwise they'll send for the other one.

**Heisenberg**   Diebner. Very possibly.

**Margrethe**   There's always a Diebner at hand ready to take over our crimes.

**Heisenberg**   Diebner might manage to get a little further than me.

**Bohr**   Diebner?

**Heisenberg**   Might. Just possibly might.

**Bohr**   He hasn't a quarter of your ability!

**Heisenberg**   Not a tenth of it. But he has ten times the eagerness to do it. It might be a very different story if it's Diebner who puts the case at our meeting with Albert Speer, instead of me.

**Margrethe**   The famous meeting with Speer.

**Heisenberg**   But this is when it counts. This is the real moment of decision. It's June 1942. Nine months after my trip to Copenhagen. All research cancelled by Hitler unless it produces immediate results – and Speer is the sole arbiter of what will qualify. Now, we've just got the first sign that our reactor's going to work. Our first increase in neutrons. Not much – thirteen per cent – but it's a start.

**Bohr**   June 1942? You're slightly ahead of Fermi in Chicago.

**Heisenberg**   Only we don't know that. But the RAF have begun terror-bombing. They've obliterated half of Lübeck, and the whole centre of Rostock and Cologne. We're desperate for new weapons to strike back with. If ever there's a moment to make our case, this is it.

**Margrethe**   You don't ask him for the funding to continue?

**Heisenberg**   To continue with the reactor? Of course I do. But I ask for so little that he doesn't take the programme seriously.

**Margrethe**   Do you tell him the reactor will produce plutonium?

**Heisenberg**   I don't tell him the reactor will produce plutonium. Not Speer, no. I don't tell him the reactor will produce plutonium.

**Bohr**   A striking omission, I have to admit.

**Heisenberg**   And what happens? It works! He gives us barely enough money to keep the reactor programme ticking over. And that is the end of the German atomic bomb. That is the end of it.

**Margrethe**   You go on with the reactor, though.

**Heisenberg**   We go on with the reactor. Of course. Because now there's no risk of getting it running in time to produce enough plutonium for a bomb. No, we go on with the reactor all right. We work like madmen on the reactor. We have to drag it all the way across Germany, from east to west, from Berlin to Swabia, to get it away from the bombing, to keep it out of the hands of the Russians. Diebner tries to hijack it on the way. We get it away from him, and we set it up in a little village in the Swabian Jura.

**Bohr**   This is Haigerloch?

**Heisenberg**   There's a natural shelter there – the village inn has a wine-cellar cut into the base of a cliff. We dig a hole in the floor for the reactor, and I keep that programme going, I keep it under my control, until the bitter end.

**Bohr**   But, Heisenberg, with respect now, with the greatest respect, you couldn't even keep the reactor under your control. That reactor was going to kill you.

**Heisenberg**   It wasn't put to the test. It never went critical.

**Bohr**   Thank God. Hambro and Perrin examined it after the Allied troops took over. They said it had no cadmium control rods. There was nothing to absorb any excess of neutrons, to slow the reaction down when it overheated.

**Heisenberg**   No rods, no.

**Bohr**   You believed the reaction would be self-limiting.

**Heisenberg**   That's what I originally believed.

**Bohr**   Heisenberg, the reaction would not have been self-limiting.

**Heisenberg**   By 1945 I understood that.

**Bohr**   So if you ever had got it to go critical, it would have melted down, and vanished into the centre of the earth!

**Heisenberg**   Not at all. We had a lump of cadmium to hand.

**Bohr**   A *lump* of cadmium? What were you proposing to do with a *lump* of cadmium?

**Heisenberg**   Throw it into the water.

**Bohr**   What water?

**Heisenberg**   The heavy water. The moderator that the uranium was immersed in.

**Bohr**   My dear good Heisenberg, not to criticise, but you'd all gone mad!

**Heisenberg**   We were almost there! We had this fantastic neutron growth! We had 670 per cent growth!

**Bohr**   You'd lost all contact with reality down in that hole!

**Heisenberg**   Another week. Another fortnight. That's all we needed!

**Bohr**  It was only the arrival of the Allies that saved you!

**Heisenberg**  We'd almost reached the critical mass! A tiny bit bigger and the chain would sustain itself indefinitely. All we need is a little more uranium. I set off with Weizsäcker to try and get our hands on Diebner's. Another hair-raising journey all the way back across Germany. Constant air raids – no trains – we try bicycles – we never make it! We end up stuck in a little inn somewhere in the middle of nowhere, listening to the thump of bombs falling all round us. And on the radio someone playing the Beethoven G minor cello sonata . . .

**Bohr**  And everything was still under your control?

**Heisenberg**  Under my control – yes! That's the point! Under my control!

**Bohr**  Nothing was under anyone's control by that time!

**Heisenberg**  Yes, because at last we were free of all constraints! The nearer the end came the faster we could work!

**Bohr**  You were no longer running that programme, Heisenberg. The programme was running you.

**Heisenberg**  Two more weeks, two more blocks of uranium, and it would have been German physics that achieved the world's first self-sustaining chain reaction.

**Bohr**  Except that Fermi had already done it in Chicago, two years earlier.

**Heisenberg**  We didn't know that.

**Bohr**  You didn't know anything down in that cave. You were as blind as moles in a hole. Perrin said that there wasn't even anything to protect you all from the radiation.

**Heisenberg**  We didn't have time to think about it.

**Bohr**  So if it *had* gone critical . . .

**Margrethe**  You'd all have died of radiation sickness.

**Bohr**   My dear Heisenberg! My dear boy!

**Heisenberg**   Yes, but by then the reactor would have been running.

**Bohr**   I should have been there to look after you.

**Heisenberg**   That's all we could think of at the time. To get the reactor running, to get the reactor running.

**Bohr**   You always needed me there to slow you down a little. Your own walking lump of cadmium.

**Heisenberg**   If I had died then, what should I have missed? Thirty years of attempting to explain. Thirty years of reproach and hostility. Even you turned your back on me.

**Margrethe**   You came to Copenhagen again. You came to Tisvilde.

**Heisenberg**   It was never the same.

**Bohr**   No. It was never the same.

**Heisenberg**   I sometimes think that those final few weeks at Haigerloch were the last happy time in my life. In a strange way it was very peaceful. Suddenly we were out of all the politics of Berlin. Out of the bombing. The war was coming to an end. There was nothing to think about except the reactor. And we didn't go mad, in fact. We didn't work all the time. There was a monastery on top of the rock above our cave. I used to retire to the organ-loft in the church, and play Bach fugues.

**Margrethe**   Look at him. He's lost. He's like a lost child. He's been out in the woods all day, running here, running there. He's shown off, he's been brave, he's been cowardly. He's done wrong, he's done right. And now the evening's come, and all he wants is to go home, and he's lost.

**Heisenberg**   Silence.

**Bohr**   Silence.

**Margrethe**   Silence.

**Heisenberg**   And once again the tiller slams over, and Christian is falling.

**Bohr**   Once again he's struggling towards the lifebuoy.

**Margrethe**   Once again I look up from my work, and there's Niels in the doorway, silently watching me ...

**Bohr**   So, Heisenberg, why did you come to Copenhagen in 1941? It was right that you told us about all the fears you had. But you didn't really think I'd tell you whether the Americans were working on a bomb.

**Heisenberg**   No.

**Bohr**   You didn't seriously hope that I'd stop them.

**Heisenberg**   No.

**Bohr**   You were going back to work on that reactor whatever I said.

**Heisenberg**   Yes.

**Bohr**   So, Heisenberg, why did you come?

**Heisenberg**   Why did I come?

**Bohr**   Tell us once again. Another draft of the paper. And this time we shall get it right. This time we shall understand.

**Margrethe**   Maybe you'll even understand yourself.

**Bohr**   After all, the workings of the atom were difficult to explain. We made many attempts. Each time we tried they became more obscure. We got there in the end, however. So – another draft, another draft.

**Heisenberg**   Why did I come? And once again I go through that evening in 1941. I crunch over the familiar gravel, and tug at the familiar bell-pull. What's in my head? Fear, certainly, and the absurd and horrible importance of someone bearing bad news. But ... yes ... something else as well. Here it comes again. I can almost see its face. Something good. Something bright and eager and hopeful.

**Bohr**   I open the door . . .

**Heisenberg**   And there he is. I see his eyes light up at the sight of me.

**Bohr**   He's smiling his wary schoolboy smile.

**Heisenberg**   And I feel a moment of such consolation.

**Bohr**   A flash of such pure gladness.

**Heisenberg**   As if I'd come home after a long journey.

**Bohr**   As if a long-lost child had appeared on the doorstep.

**Heisenberg**   Suddenly I'm free of all the dark tangled currents in the water.

**Bohr**   Christian is alive, Harald still unborn.

**Heisenberg**   The world is at peace again.

**Margrethe**   Look at them. Father and son still. Just for a moment. Even now we're all dead.

**Bohr**   For a moment, yes, it's the twenties again.

**Heisenberg**   And we shall speak to each other and understand each other in the way we did before.

**Margrethe**   And from those two heads the future will emerge. Which cities will be destroyed, and which survive. Who will die, and who will live. Which world will go down to obliteration, and which will triumph.

**Bohr**   My dear Heisenberg!

**Heisenberg**   My dear Bohr!

**Bohr**   Come in, come in . . .

# Act Two

**Heisenberg** It was the very beginning of spring. The first time I came to Copenhagen, in 1924. March: raw, blustery northern weather. But every now and then the sun would come out and leave that first marvellous warmth of the year on your skin. That first breath of returning life.

**Bohr** You were twenty-two. So I must have been . . .

**Heisenberg** Thirty-eight.

**Bohr** Almost the same age as you were when you came in 1941.

**Heisenberg** So what do we do?

**Bohr** Put on our boots and rucksacks . . .

**Heisenberg** Take the tram to the end of the line . . .

**Bohr** And start walking!

**Heisenberg** Northwards to Elsinore.

**Bohr** If you walk you talk.

**Heisenberg** Then westwards to Tisvilde.

**Bohr** And back by way of Hillerød.

**Heisenberg** Walking, talking, for a hundred miles.

**Bohr** After which we talked more or less non-stop for the next three years.

**Heisenberg** We'd split a bottle of wine over dinner in your flat at the Institute.

**Bohr** Then I'd come up to your room . . .

**Heisenberg** That terrible little room in the servants' quarters in the attic.

**Bohr** And we'd talk on into the small hours.

**Heisenberg**  How, though?

**Bohr**  How?

**Heisenberg**  How did we talk? In Danish?

**Bohr**  In German, surely.

**Heisenberg**  I lectured in Danish. I had to give my first colloquium when I'd only been here for ten weeks.

**Bohr**  I remember it. Your Danish was already excellent.

**Heisenberg**  No. You did a terrible thing to me. Half-an-hour before it started you said casually, Oh, I think we'll speak English today.

**Bohr**  But when you explained . . . ?

**Heisenberg**  Explain to the Pope? I didn't dare. That excellent Danish you heard was my first attempt at English.

**Bohr**  My dear Heisenberg! On our own together, though? My love, do you recall?

**Margrethe**  What language you spoke when I wasn't there? You think I had microphones hidden?

**Bohr**  No, no – but patience, my love, patience!

**Margrethe**  Patience?

**Bohr**  You sounded a little sharp.

**Margrethe**  Not at all.

**Bohr**  We have to follow the threads right back to the beginning of the maze.

**Margrethe**  I'm watching every step.

**Bohr**  You didn't mind? I hope.

**Margrethe**  Mind?

**Bohr**  Being left at home?

**Margrethe**  While you went off on your hike? Of course not. Why should I have minded? You had to get out of the

house. Two new sons arriving on top of each other would
be rather a lot for any man to put up with.

**Bohr**   Two new sons?

**Margrethe**   Heisenberg.

**Bohr**   Yes, yes.

**Margrethe**   And our own son.

**Bohr**   Aage?

**Margrethe**   Ernest!

**Bohr**   1924 – of course – Ernest.

**Margrethe**   Number five. Yes?

**Bohr**   Yes, yes, yes. And if it was March, you're right –
he couldn't have been much more than . . .

**Margrethe**   One week.

**Bohr**   One week? One week, yes. And you really didn't
mind?

**Margrethe**   Not at all. I was pleased you had an excuse
to get away. And you always went off hiking with your new
assistants. You went off with Kramers, when he arrived in
1916.

**Bohr**   Yes, when I suppose Christian was still only . . .

**Margrethe**   One week.

**Bohr**   Yes. . . . Yes. . . . I almost killed Kramers, you
know.

**Heisenberg**   Not with a cap-pistol?

**Bohr**   With a mine. On our walk.

**Heisenberg**   Oh, the mine. Yes, you told me, on ours.
Never mind Kramers – you almost killed yourself!

**Bohr**   A mine washed up in the shallows . . .

**Heisenberg**   And of course at once they compete to throw stones at it. What were you thinking of?

**Bohr**   I've no idea.

**Heisenberg**   A touch of Elsinore there, perhaps.

**Bohr**   Elsinore?

**Heisenberg**   The darkness inside the human soul.

**Bohr**   You did something just as idiotic.

**Heisenberg**   *I* did?

**Bohr**   With Dirac in Japan. You climbed a pagoda.

**Heisenberg**   Oh, the pagoda.

**Bohr**   Then balanced on the pinnacle. According to Dirac. On one foot. In a high wind. I'm glad I wasn't there.

**Heisenberg**   Elsinore, I confess.

**Bohr**   Elsinore, certainly.

**Heisenberg**   I was jealous of Kramers, you know.

**Bohr**   His Eminence. Isn't that what you called him?

**Heisenberg**   Because that's what he was. Your leading cardinal. Your favourite son. Till I arrived on the scene.

**Margrethe**   He was a wonderful cellist.

**Bohr**   He was a wonderful everything.

**Heisenberg**   Far too wonderful.

**Margrethe**   I liked him.

**Heisenberg**   I was terrified of him. When I first started at the Institute. I was terrified of all of them. All the boy wonders you had here – they were all so brilliant and accomplished. But Kramers was the heir apparent. All the rest of us had to work in the general study hall. Kramers had the private office next to yours, like the electron on the inmost orbit around the nucleus. And he didn't think much of my physics. He insisted you could explain everything about the atom by classical mechanics.

**Bohr**    Well, he was wrong.

**Margrethe**    And very soon the private office was vacant.

**Bohr**    And there was another electron on the inmost orbit.

**Heisenberg**    Yes, and for three years we lived inside the atom.

**Bohr**    With other electrons on the outer orbits around us all over Europe.

**Heisenberg**    Max Born and Pascual Jordan in Göttingen.

**Bohr**    Yes, but Schrödinger in Zürich, Fermi in Rome.

**Heisenberg**    Chadwick and Dirac in England.

**Bohr**    Joliot and de Broglie in Paris.

**Heisenberg**    Gamow and Landau in Russia.

**Bohr**    Everyone in and out of each other's departments.

**Heisenberg**    Papers and drafts of papers on every international mail-train.

**Bohr**    You remember when Goudsmit and Uhlenbeck did spin?

**Heisenberg**    There's this one last variable in the quantum state of the atom that no one can make sense of. The last hurdle . . .

**Bohr**    And these two crazy Dutchmen go back to a ridiculous idea that electrons can spin in different ways.

**Heisenberg**    And of course the first thing that everyone wants to know is, What line is Copenhagen going to take?

**Bohr**    I'm on my way to Leiden, as it happens.

**Heisenberg**    And it turns into a papal progress! The train stops on the way at Hamburg . . .

**Bohr**    Pauli and Stern are waiting on the platform to ask me what I think about spin.

**Heisenberg**  You tell them it's wrong.

**Bohr**  No, I tell them it's very . . .

**Heisenberg**  Interesting.

**Bohr**  I think that is precisely the word I choose.

**Heisenberg**  Then the train pulls into Leiden.

**Bohr**  And I'm met at the barrier by Einstein and Ehrenfest. And I change my mind because Einstein – Einstein, you see? – I'm the Pope – he's God – because Einstein has made a relativistic analysis, and it resolves all my doubts.

**Heisenberg**  Meanwhile I'm standing in for Max Born at Göttingen, so you make a detour there on your way home.

**Bohr**  And you and Jordan meet me at the station.

**Heisenberg**  Same question: what do you think of spin?

**Bohr**  And when the train stops at Berlin there's Pauli on the platform.

**Heisenberg**  Wolfgang Pauli, who never gets out of bed if he can possibly avoid it . . .

**Bohr**  And who's already met me once at Hamburg on the journey out . . .

**Heisenberg**  He's travelled all the way from Hamburg to Berlin purely in order to see you for the second time round . . .

**Bohr**  And find out how my ideas on spin have developed en route.

**Heisenberg**  Oh, those years! Those amazing years! Those three short years!

**Bohr**  From 1924 to 1927.

**Heisenberg**  From when I arrived in Copenhagen to work with you . . .

**Bohr**   To when you departed, to take up your chair at Leipzig.

**Heisenberg**   Three years of raw, bracing northern springtime.

**Bohr**   At the end of which we had quantum mechanics, we had uncertainty . . .

**Heisenberg**   We had complementarity . . .

**Bohr**   We had the whole Copenhagen Interpretation.

**Heisenberg**   Europe in all its glory again. A new Enlightenment, with Germany back in her rightful place at the heart of it. And who led the way for everyone else?

**Margrethe**   You and Niels.

**Heisenberg**   Well, we did.

**Bohr**   We did.

**Margrethe**   And that's what you were trying to get back to in 1941?

**Heisenberg**   To something we did in those three years. . . . Something we said, something we thought. . . . I keep almost seeing it out of the corner of my eye as we talk! Something about the way we worked. Something about the way we did all those things . . .

**Bohr**   Together.

**Heisenberg**   Together. Yes, together.

**Margrethe**   No.

**Bohr**   No? What do you mean, no?

**Margrethe**   Not together. You didn't do any of those things together.

**Bohr**   Yes, we did. Of course we did.

**Margrethe**   No, you didn't. Every single one of them you did when you were apart. *You* first worked out quantum mechanics on Heligoland.

**Heisenberg**   Well, it was summer by then. I had my hay fever.

**Margrethe**   And on Heligoland, on your own, on a rocky bare island in the middle of the North Sea, you said there was nothing to distract you . . .

**Heisenberg**   My head began to clear, and I had this very sharp picture of what atomic physics ought to be like. I suddenly realised that we had to limit it to the measurements we could actually make, to what we could actually observe. We can't see the electrons inside the atom . . .

**Margrethe**   Any more than Niels can see the thoughts in your head, or you the thoughts in Niels's.

**Heisenberg**   All we can see are the effects that the electrons produce, on the light that they reflect . . .

**Bohr**   But the difficulties you were trying to resolve were the ones we'd explored together, over dinner in the flat, on the beach at Tisvilde.

**Heisenberg**   Of course. But I remember the evening when the mathematics first began to chime with the principle.

**Margrethe**   On Heligoland.

**Heisenberg**   On Heligoland.

**Margrethe**   On your own.

**Heisenberg**   It was terribly laborious – I didn't understand matrix calculus then . . . I get so excited I keep making mistakes. But by three in the morning I've got it. I seem to be looking through the surface of atomic phenomena into a strangely beautiful interior world. A world of pure mathematical structures. I'm too excited to sleep. I go down to the southern end of the island. There's a rock jutting out into the sea that I've been longing to climb. I get up it in the half-light before the dawn, and lie on top, gazing out to sea.

**Margrethe**  On your own.

**Heisenberg**  On my own. And yes – I was happy.

**Margrethe**  Happier than you were back here with us all in Copenhagen the following winter.

**Heisenberg**  What, with all the Schrödinger nonsense?

**Bohr**  Nonsense? Come, come. Schrödinger's wave formulation?

**Margrethe**  Yes, suddenly everyone's turned their backs on your wonderful new matrix mechanics.

**Heisenberg**  No one can understand it.

**Margrethe**  And they *can* understand Schrödinger's wave mechanics.

**Heisenberg**  Because they'd learnt it in school! We're going backwards to classical physics! And when I'm a little cautious about accepting it . . .

**Bohr**  A little cautious? Not to criticise, but . . .

**Margrethe**  . . . You described it as repulsive!

**Heisenberg**  I said the physical implications were repulsive. Schrödinger said my mathematics were repulsive.

**Bohr**  I seem to recall you used the word . . . well, I won't repeat it in mixed company.

**Heisenberg**  In private. But by that time people had gone crazy.

**Margrethe**  They thought you were simply jealous.

**Heisenberg**  Someone even suggested some bizarre kind of intellectual snobbery. You got extremely excited.

**Bohr**  On your behalf.

**Heisenberg**  You invited Schrödinger here . . .

**Bohr**    To have a calm debate about our differences.

**Heisenberg**    And you fell on him like a madman. You meet him at the station – of course – and you pitch into him before he's even got his bags off the train. Then you go on at him from first thing in the morning until last thing at night.

**Bohr**    *I* go on? *He* goes on!

**Heisenberg**    Because you won't make the least concession!

**Bohr**    Nor will he!

**Heisenberg**    You made him ill! He had to retire to bed to get away from you!

**Bohr**    He had a slight feverish cold.

**Heisenberg**    Margrethe had to nurse him!

**Margrethe**    I dosed him with tea and cake to keep his strength up.

**Heisenberg**    Yes, while you pursued him even into the sickroom! Sat on his bed and hammered away at him!

**Bohr**    Perfectly politely.

**Heisenberg**    You were the Pope and the Holy Office and the Inquisition all rolled into one! And then, and then, after Schrödinger had fled back to Zürich – and this I will never forget, Bohr, this I will never let you forget – you started to take his side! You turned on me!

**Bohr**    Because *you'd* gone mad by this time! You'd become fanatical! You were refusing to allow wave theory any place in quantum mechanics at all!

**Heisenberg**    You'd completely turned your coat!

**Bohr**    I said wave mechanics and matrix mechanics were simply alternative tools.

**Heisenberg**    Something you're always accusing me of. 'If it works it works.' Never mind what it means.

**Bohr**  Of course I mind what it means.

**Heisenberg**  What it means in language.

**Bohr**  In plain language, yes.

**Heisenberg**  What something means is what it means in mathematics.

**Bohr**  You think that so long as the mathematics works out, the sense doesn't matter.

**Heisenberg**  Mathematics *is* sense! That's what sense is!

**Bohr**  But in the end, in the end, remember, we have to be able to explain it all to Margrethe!

**Margrethe**  Explain it to me? You couldn't even explain it to each other! You went on arguing into the small hours every night! You both got so angry!

**Bohr**  We also both got completely exhausted.

**Margrethe**  It was the cloud chamber that finished you.

**Bohr**  Yes, because if you detach an electron from an atom, and send it through a cloud chamber, you can see the track it leaves.

**Heisenberg**  And it's a scandal. There shouldn't be a track!

**Margrethe**  According to your quantum mechanics.

**Heisenberg**  There *isn't* a track! No orbits! No tracks or trajectories! Only external effects!

**Margrethe**  Only there the track is. I've seen it myself, as clear as the wake left by a passing ship.

**Bohr**  It was a fascinating paradox.

**Heisenberg**  You actually loved the paradoxes, that's your problem. You revelled in the contradictions.

**Bohr**  Yes, and you've never been able to understand the suggestiveness of paradox and contradiction. That's *your* problem. You live and breathe paradox and contradiction, but you can no more see the beauty of them than the fish can see the beauty of the water.

**Heisenberg**   I sometimes felt as if I was trapped in a kind of windowless hell. You don't realise how aggressive you are. Prowling up and down the room as if you're going to eat someone – and I can guess who it's going to be.

**Bohr**   That's the way we did the physics, though.

**Margrethe**   No. No! In the end you did it on your own again! Even you! You went off ski-ing in Norway.

**Bohr**   I had to get away from it all!

**Margrethe**   And you worked out complementarity in Norway, on your own.

**Heisenberg**   The speed he skis at he had to do *something* to keep the blood going round. It was either physics or frostbite.

**Bohr**   Yes, and you stayed behind in Copenhagen . . .

**Heisenberg**   And started to think at last.

**Margrethe**   You're a lot better off apart, you two.

**Heisenberg**   Having him out of town was as liberating as getting away from my hay fever on Heligoland.

**Margrethe**   I shouldn't let you sit anywhere near each other, if I were the teacher.

**Heisenberg**   And that's when I did uncertainty. Walking round Faelled Park on my own one horrible raw February night. It's very late, and as soon as I've turned off into the park I'm completely alone in the darkness. I start to think about what you'd see, if you could train a telescope on me from the mountains of Norway. You'd see me by the street-lamps on the Blegdamsvej, then nothing as I vanished into the darkness, then another glimpse of me as I passed the lamp-post in front of the bandstand. And that's what we see in the cloud chamber. Not a continuous track but a series of glimpses – a series of collisions between the

passing electron and various molecules of water vapour. . . .
Or think of you, on your great papal progress to Leiden in
1925. What did Margrethe see of that, at home here in
Copenhagen? A picture postcard from Hamburg, perhaps.
Then one from Leiden. One from Göttingen. One from
Berlin. Because what we see in the cloud chamber are not
even the collisions themselves, but the water-droplets that
condense around them, as big as cities around a traveller –
no, vastly bigger still, relatively – complete countries –
Germany . . . Holland . . . Germany again. There is no
track, there are no precise addresses; only a vague list of
countries visited. I don't know why we hadn't thought of it
before, except that we were too busy arguing to think at
all.

**Bohr**    You seem to have given up on all forms of
discussion. By the time I get back from Norway I find
you've done a draft of your uncertainty paper and you've
already sent it for publication!

**Margrethe**    And an even worse battle begins.

**Bohr**    My dear good Heisenberg, it's not open behaviour
to rush a first draft into print before we've discussed it
together! It's not the way we work!

**Heisenberg**    No, the way we work is that you hound me
from first thing in the morning till last thing at night! The
way we work is that you drive me mad!

**Bohr**    Yes, because the paper contains a fundamental
error.

**Margrethe**    And here we go again.

**Heisenberg**    No, but I show him the strangest truth
about the universe that any of us has stumbled on since
relativity – that you can never know everything about the
whereabouts of a particle, or anything else, even Bohr now,
as he prowls up and down the room in that maddening
way of his, because we can't observe it without introducing
some new element into the situation, a molecule of water
vapour for it to hit, or a piece of light – things which have

an energy of their own, and which therefore have an effect on what they hit. A small one, admittedly, in the case of Bohr . . .

**Bohr**    Yes, if you know where I am with the kind of accuracy we're talking about when we're dealing with particles, you can still measure my velocity to within – what . . .?

**Heisenberg**    Something like a billionth of a billionth of a kilometre per second. The theoretical point remains, though, that you have no absolutely determinate situation in the world, which among other things lays waste to the idea of causality, the whole foundation of science – because if you don't know how things are today you certainly can't know how they're going to be tomorrow. I shatter the objective universe around you – and all you can say is that there's an error in the formulation!

**Bohr**    There is!

**Margrethe**    Tea, anyone? Cake?

**Heisenberg**    Listen, in my paper what we're trying to locate is not a free electron off on its travels through a cloud chamber, but an electron when it's at home, moving around inside an atom . . .

**Bohr**    And the uncertainty arises not, as you claim, through its indeterminate recoil when it's hit by an incoming photon . . .

**Heisenberg**    Plain language, plain language!

**Bohr**    This *is* plain language.

**Heisenberg**    Listen . . .

**Bohr**    The language of classical mechanics.

**Heisenberg**    Listen! Copenhagen is an atom. Margrethe is its nucleus. About right, the scale? Ten thousand to one?

**Bohr**    Yes, yes.

**Heisenberg**    Now, Bohr's an electron. He's wandering

about the city somewhere in the darkness, no one knows where. He's here, he's there, he's everywhere and nowhere. Up in Faelled Park, down at Carlsberg. Passing City Hall, out by the harbour. I'm a photon. A quantum of light. I'm despatched into the darkness to find Bohr. And I succeed, because I manage to collide with him. . . . But what's happened? Look – he's been slowed down, he's been deflected! He's no longer doing exactly what he was so maddeningly doing when I walked into him!

**Bohr**    But, Heisenberg, Heisenberg! You also have been deflected! If people can see what's happened to you, to their piece of light, then they can work out what must have happened to me! The trouble is knowing what's happened to you! Because to understand how people see you we have to treat you not just as a particle, but as a wave. I have to use not only your particle mechanics, I have to use the Schrödinger wave function.

**Heisenberg**    I know – I put it in a postscript to my paper.

**Bohr**    Everyone remembers the paper – no one remembers the postscript. But the question is fundamental. Particles are things, complete in themselves. Waves are disturbances in something else.

**Heisenberg**    I know. Complementarity. It's in the postscript.

**Bohr**    They're either one thing or the other. They can't be both. We have to choose one way of seeing them or the other. But as soon as we do we can't know everything about them.

**Heisenberg**    And off he goes into orbit again. Incidentally exemplifying another application of complementarity. Exactly where you go as you ramble around is of course completely determined by your genes and the various physical forces acting on you. But it's also completely determined by your own entirely inscrutable whims from one moment to the next. So we can't completely understand your behaviour without seeing it both ways at once, and that's impossible. Which means that your extraordinary peregrinations are not fully objective aspects of the universe. They exist only partially, through the efforts of me or Margrethe, as our minds shift endlessly back and forth between the two approaches.

**Bohr**   You've never absolutely and totally accepted complementarity, have you?

**Heisenberg**   Yes! Absolutely and totally! I defended it at the Como Conference in 1927! I have adhered to it ever afterwards with religious fervour! You convinced me. I humbly accepted your criticisms.

**Bohr**   Not before you'd said some deeply wounding things.

**Heisenberg**   Good God, at one point you literally reduced me to tears!

**Bohr**   Forgive me, but I diagnosed them as tears of frustration and rage.

**Heisenberg**   I was having a tantrum?

**Bohr**   I have brought up children of my own.

**Heisenberg**   And what about Margrethe? Was *she* having a tantrum? Klein told me you reduced *her* to tears after I'd gone, making her type out your endless redraftings of the complementarity paper.

**Bohr**   I don't recall that.

**Margrethe**   I do.

**Heisenberg**   We had to drag Pauli out of bed in Hamburg once again to come to Copenhagen and negotiate peace.

**Bohr**   He succeeded. We ended up with a treaty. Uncertainty and complementarity became the two central tenets of the Copenhagen Interpretation of Quantum Mechanics.

**Heisenberg**    A political compromise, of course, like most treaties.

**Bohr**    You see? Somewhere inside you there are still secret reservations.

**Heisenberg**    Not at all – it works. That's what matters. It works, it works, it works!

**Bohr**    It works, yes. But it's more important than that. Because you see what we did in those three years, Heisenberg? Not to exaggerate, but we turned the world inside out! Yes, listen, now it comes, now it comes. . . . We put man back at the centre of the universe. Throughout history we keep finding ourselves displaced. We keep exiling ourselves to the periphery of things. First we turn ourselves into a mere adjunct of God's unknowable purposes, tiny figures kneeling in the great cathedral of creation. And no sooner have we recovered ourselves in the Renaissance, no sooner has man become, as Protagoras proclaimed him, the measure of all things, than we're pushed aside again by the products of our own reasoning! We're dwarfed again as physicists build the great new cathedrals for us to wonder at – the laws of classical mechanics that pre-date us from the beginning of eternity, that will survive us to eternity's end, that exist whether we exist or not. Until we come to the beginning of the twentieth century, and we're suddenly forced to rise from our knees again.

**Heisenberg**    It starts with Einstein.

**Bohr**    It starts with Einstein. He shows that measurement – measurement, on which the whole possibility of science depends – measurement is not an impersonal event that occurs with impartial universality. It's a human act, carried out from a specific point of view in time and space, from the one particular viewpoint of a possible observer. Then, here in Copenhagen in those three years in the mid-twenties we discover that there is no precisely determinable objective universe. That the universe exists only as a series of approximations. Only within the limits determined by our relationship with it. Only through the understanding lodged inside the human head.

**Margrethe**   So this man you've put at the centre of the universe – is it you, or is it Heisenberg?

**Bohr**   Now, now, my love.

**Margrethe**   Yes, but it makes a difference.

**Bohr**   Either of us. Both of us. Yourself. All of us.

**Margrethe**   If it's Heisenberg at the centre of the universe, then the one bit of the universe that he can't see is Heisenberg.

**Heisenberg**   So . . .

**Margrethe**   So it's no good asking him why he came to Copenhagen in 1941. He doesn't know!

**Heisenberg**   I thought for a moment just then I caught a glimpse of it.

**Margrethe**   Then you turned to look.

**Heisenberg**   And away it went.

**Margrethe**   Complementarity again. Yes?

**Bohr**   Yes, yes.

**Margrethe**   I've typed it out often enough. If you're doing something you have to concentrate on you can't also be thinking about doing it, and if you're thinking about doing it then you can't actually be doing it. Yes?

**Heisenberg**   Swerve left, swerve right, or think about it and die.

**Bohr**   But *after* you've done it . . .

**Margrethe**   You look back and make a guess, just like the rest of us. Only a worse guess, because you didn't see yourself doing it, and we did. Forgive me, but you don't even know why you did uncertainty in the first place.

**Bohr**  Whereas if *you're* the one at the centre of the universe . . .

**Margrethe**  Then I can tell you that it was because you wanted to drop a bomb on Schrödinger.

**Heisenberg**  I wanted to show he was wrong, certainly.

**Margrethe**  And Schrödinger was winning the war. When the Leipzig chair first became vacant that autumn he was short-listed for it and you weren't. You needed a wonderful new weapon.

**Bohr**  Not to criticise, Margrethe, but you have a tendency to make everything personal.

**Margrethe**  Because everything *is* personal! You've just read us all a lecture about it! You know how much Heisenberg wanted a chair. You know the pressure he was under from his family. I'm sorry, but you want to make everything seem heroically abstract and logical. And when you tell the story, yes, it all falls into place, it all has a beginning and a middle and an end. But I was there, and when I remember what it was like I'm there still, and I look around me and what I see isn't a story! It's confusion and rage and jealousy and tears and no one knowing what things mean or which way they're going to go.

**Heisenberg**  All the same, it works, it works.

**Margrethe**  Yes, it works wonderfully. Within three months of publishing your uncertainty paper you're offered Leipzig.

**Heisenberg**  I didn't mean that.

**Margrethe**  Not to mention somewhere else and somewhere else.

**Heisenberg**  Halle and Munich and Zürich.

**Bohr**  And various American universities.

**Heisenberg**  But I didn't mean that.

**Margrethe**    And when you take up your chair at Leipzig you're how old?

**Heisenberg**    Twenty-six.

**Bohr**    The youngest full professor in Germany.

**Heisenberg**    I mean the Copenhagen Interpretation. The Copenhagen Interpretation works. However we got there, by whatever combination of high principles and low calculation, of most painfully hard thought and most painfully childish tears, it works. It goes on working.

**Margrethe**    Yes, and why did you both accept the Interpretation in the end? Was it really because you wanted to re-establish humanism?

**Bohr**    Of course not. It was because it was the only way to explain what the experimenters had observed.

**Margrethe**    Or was it because now you were becoming a professor you wanted a solidly established doctrine to teach? Because you wanted to have your new ideas publicly endorsed by the head of the church in Copenhagen? And perhaps Niels agreed to endorse them in return for your accepting *his* doctrines. For recognising him as head of the church. And if you want to know why you came to Copenhagen in 1941 I'll tell you that as well. You're right – there's no great mystery about it. You came to show yourself off to us.

**Bohr**    Margrethe!

**Margrethe**    No! When he first came in 1924 he was a humble assistant lecturer from a humiliated nation, grateful to have a job. Now here you are, back in triumph – the leading scientist in a nation that's conquered most of Europe. You've come to show us how well you've done in life.

**Bohr**    This is so unlike you!

**Margrethe**    I'm sorry, but isn't that really why he's here? Because he's burning to let us know that he's in charge of some vital piece of secret research. And that even so he's preserved a lofty moral independence. Preserved it so famously that he's being watched by the Gestapo. Preserved it so successfully that he's now also got a wonderfully important moral dilemma to face.

**Bohr**  Yes, well, now you're simply working yourself up.

**Margrethe**  A chain reaction. You tell one painful truth and it leads to two more. And as you frankly admit, you're going to go back and continue doing precisely what you were doing before, whatever Niels tells you.

**Heisenberg**  Yes.

**Margrethe**  Because you wouldn't dream of giving up such a wonderful opportunity for research.

**Heisenberg**  Not if I can possibly help it.

**Margrethe**  Also you want to demonstrate to the Nazis how useful theoretical physics can be. You want to save the honour of German science. You want to be there to re-establish it in all its glory as soon as the war's over.

**Heisenberg**  All the same, I don't tell Speer that the reactor . . .

**Margrethe**  . . . will produce plutonium, no, because you're afraid of what will happen if the Nazis commit huge resources, and you fail to deliver the bombs. Please don't try to tell us that you're a hero of the resistance.

**Heisenberg**  I've never claimed to be a hero.

**Margrethe**  Your talent is for ski-ing too fast for anyone to see where you are. For always being in more than one position at a time, like one of your particles.

**Heisenberg**  I can only say that it worked. Unlike most of the gestures made by heroes of the resistance. It worked! I know what you think. You think I should have joined the plot against Hitler, and got myself hanged like the others.

**Bohr**  Of course not.

**Heisenberg**   You don't say it, because there are some things that can't be said. But you think it.

**Bohr**   No.

**Heisenberg**   What would it have achieved? What would it have achieved if you'd dived in after Christian, and drowned as well? But that's another thing that can't be said.

**Bohr**   Only thought.

**Heisenberg**   Yes. I'm sorry.

**Bohr**   And rethought. Every day.

**Heisenberg**   You had to be held back, I know.

**Margrethe**   Whereas you held yourself back.

**Heisenberg**   Better to stay on the boat, though, and fetch it about. Better to remain alive, and throw the lifebuoy. Surely!

**Bohr**   Perhaps. Perhaps not.

**Heisenberg**   Better. Better.

**Margrethe**   Really it is ridiculous. You reasoned your way, both of you, with such astonishing delicacy and precision into the tiny world of the atom. Now it turns out that everything depends upon these really rather large objects on our shoulders. And what's going on in there is . . .

**Heisenberg**   Elsinore.

**Margrethe**   Elsinore, yes.

**Heisenberg**   And you may be right. I *was* afraid of what would happen. I *was* conscious of being on the winning side. . . So many explanations for everything I did! So many of them sitting round the lunch-table! Somewhere at the head of the table, I think, is the real reason I came

to Copenhagen. Again I turn to look. . . . And for a
moment I almost see its face. Then next time I look the
chair at the head of the table is completely empty. There's
no reason at all. I didn't tell Speer simply because I didn't
think of it. I came to Copenhagen simply because I did
think of it. A million things we might do or might not do
every day. A million decisions that make themselves. Why
didn't you kill me?

**Bohr**  Why didn't I . . . ?

**Heisenberg**  Kill me. Murder me. That evening in 1941.
Here we are, walking back towards the house, and you've
just leapt to the conclusion that I'm going to arm Hitler
with nuclear weapons. You'll surely take any reasonable
steps to prevent it happening.

**Bohr**  By murdering you?

**Heisenberg**  We're in the middle of a war. I'm an
enemy. There's nothing odd or immoral about killing
enemies.

**Bohr**  I should fetch out my cap-pistol?

**Heisenberg**  You won't need your cap-pistol. You won't
even need a mine. You can do it without any loud bangs,
without any blood, without any spectacle of suffering. As
cleanly as a bomb-aimer pressing his release three thousand
metres above the earth. You simply wait till I've gone.
Then you sit quietly down in your favourite armchair here
and repeat aloud to Margrethe, in front of our unseen
audience, what I've just told you. I shall be dead almost as
soon as poor Casimir. A lot sooner than Gamow.

**Bohr**  My dear Heisenberg, the suggestion is of course . . .

**Heisenberg**  Most interesting. So interesting that it never
even occurred to you. Complementarity, once again. I'm
your enemy; I'm also your friend. I'm a danger to
mankind; I'm also your guest. I'm a particle; I'm also a
wave. We have one set of obligations to the world in
general, and we have other sets, never to be reconciled, to

our fellow-countrymen, to our neighbours, to our friends, to our family, to our children. We have to go through not two slits at the same time but twenty-two. All we can do is to look afterwards, and see what happened.

**Margrethe**  I'll tell you another reason why you did uncertainty: you have a natural affinity for it.

**Heisenberg**  Well, I must cut a gratifyingly chastened figure when I return in 1947. Crawling on my hands and knees again. My nation back in ruins.

**Margrethe**  Not really. You're demonstrating that once more you personally have come out on top.

**Heisenberg**  Begging for food parcels?

**Margrethe**  Established in Göttingen under British protection, in charge of post-war German science.

**Heisenberg**  That first year in Göttingen I slept on straw.

**Margrethe**  Elisabeth said you had a most charming house thereafter.

**Heisenberg**  I was given it by the British.

**Margrethe**  Your new foster-parents. Who'd confiscated it from someone else.

**Bohr**  Enough, my love, enough.

**Margrethe**  No, I've kept my thoughts to myself for all these years. But it's maddening to have this clever son forever dancing about in front of our eyes, forever demanding our approval, forever struggling to shock us, forever begging to be told what the limits to his freedom are, if only so that he can go out and transgress them! I'm sorry, but really. . . . On your hands and knees? It's my dear, good, kind husband who's on his hands and knees! Literally. Crawling down to the beach in the darkness in 1943, fleeing like a thief in the night from his own homeland to escape being murdered. The protection of the

German Embassy that you boasted about didn't last for long. We were incorporated into the Reich.

**Heisenberg**  I warned you in 1941. You wouldn't listen. At least Bohr got across to Sweden.

**Margrethe**  And even as the fishing-boat was taking him across the Sound two freighters were arriving in the harbour to ship the entire Jewish population of Denmark eastwards. That great darkness inside the human soul was flooding out to engulf us all.

**Heisenberg**  I did try to warn you.

**Margrethe**  Yes, and where are you? Shut away in a cave like a savage, trying to conjure an evil spirit out of a hole in the ground. That's what it came down to in the end, all that shining springtime in the 1920s, that's what it produced – a more efficient machine for killing people.

**Bohr**  It breaks my heart every time I think of it.

**Heisenberg**  It broke all our hearts.

**Margrethe**  And this wonderful machine may yet kill every man, woman, and child in the world. And if we really are the centre of the universe, if we really are all that's keeping it in being, what will be left?

**Bohr**  Darkness. Total and final darkness.

**Margrethe**  Even the questions that haunt us will at last be extinguished. Even the ghosts will die.

**Heisenberg**  I can only say that I didn't do it. I didn't build the bomb.

**Margrethe**  No, and why didn't you? I'll tell you that, too. It's the simplest reason of all. Because you couldn't. You didn't understand the physics.

**Heisenberg**  That's what Goudsmit said.

**Margrethe**  And Goudsmit knew. He was one of your magic circle. He and Uhlenbeck were the ones who did spin.

**Heisenberg**  All the same, he had no idea of what I did or didn't understand about a bomb.

**Margrethe**  He tracked you down across Europe for Allied Intelligence. He interrogated you after you were captured.

**Heisenberg**  He blamed me, of course. His parents died in Auschwitz. He thought I should have done something to save them. I don't know what. So many hands stretching up from the darkness for a lifeline, and no lifeline that could ever reach them . . .

**Margrethe**  He said you didn't understand the crucial difference between a reactor and a bomb.

**Heisenberg**  I understood very clearly. I simply didn't tell the others.

**Margrethe**  Ah.

**Heisenberg**  I understood, though.

**Margrethe**  But secretly.

**Heisenberg**  You can check if you don't believe me.

**Margrethe**  There's evidence, for once?

**Heisenberg**  It was all most carefully recorded.

**Margrethe**  Witnesses, even?

**Heisenberg**  Unimpeachable witnesses.

**Margrethe**  Who wrote it down?

**Heisenberg**  Who recorded it and transcribed it.

**Margrethe**  Even though you didn't tell anyone?

**Heisenberg**  I told one person. I told Otto Hahn. That terrible night at Farm Hall, after we'd heard the news. Somewhere in the small hours, after everyone had finally gone to bed, and we were alone together. I gave him a reasonably good account of how the bomb had worked.

**Margrethe**  After the event.

**Heisenberg**  After the event. Yes. When it didn't matter any more. All the things Goudsmit said I didn't understand. Fast neutrons in 235. The plutonium option. A reflective shell to reduce neutron escape. Even the method of triggering it.

**Bohr**  The critical mass. That was the most important thing. The amount of material you needed to establish the chain-reaction. Did you tell him the critical mass?

**Heisenberg**  I gave him a figure, yes. You can look it up! Because that was the other secret of the house-party. Diebner asked me when we first arrived if I thought there were hidden microphones. I laughed. I told him the British were far too old-fashioned to know about Gestapo methods. I underestimated them. They had microphones everywhere – they were recording everything. Look it up! Everything we said. Everything we went through that terrible night. Everything I told Hahn alone in the small hours.

**Bohr**  But the critical mass. You gave him a figure. What was the figure you gave him?

**Heisenberg**  I forget.

**Bohr**  Heisenberg . . .

**Heisenberg**  It's all on the record. You can see for yourself.

**Bohr**  The figure for the Hiroshima bomb . . .

**Heisenberg**  Was fifty kilograms.

**Bohr**  So that was the figure you gave Hahn? Fifty kilograms?

**Heisenberg**  I said about a ton.

**Bohr**  About a ton? A thousand kilograms? Heisenberg, I believe I am at last beginning to understand something.

**Heisenberg**  The one thing I was wrong about.

**Bohr**  You were twenty times over.

**Heisenberg**  The one thing.

**Bohr**  But, Heisenberg, your mathematics, your mathematics! How could they have been so far out?

**Heisenberg**  They weren't. As soon as I calculated the diffusion I got it just about right.

**Bohr**  As soon as you calculated it?

**Heisenberg**  I gave everyone a seminar on it a week later. It's in the record! Look it up!

**Bohr**  You mean . . . you hadn't calculated it before? You hadn't done the diffusion equation?

**Heisenberg**  There was no need to.

**Bohr**  No need to?

**Heisenberg**  The calculation had already been done.

**Bohr**  Done by whom?

**Heisenberg**  By Perrin and Flügge in 1939.

**Bohr**  By Perrin and Flugge? But, my dear Heisenberg, that was for natural uranium. Wheeler and I showed that it was only the 235 that fissioned.

**Heisenberg**  Your great paper. The basis of everything we did.

**Bohr**  So you needed to calculate the figure for pure 235.

**Heisenberg**  Obviously.

**Bohr**  And you didn't?

**Heisenberg**  I didn't.

**Bohr**  And that's why you were so confident you couldn't do it until you had the plutonium. Because you spent the entire war believing that it would take not a few kilograms of 235, but a ton or more. And to make a ton of 235 in any plausible time . . .

**Heisenberg**  Would have needed something like two

hundred million separator units. It was plainly unimaginable.

**Bohr** If you'd realised you had to produce only a few kilograms . . .

**Heisenberg** Even to make a single kilogram would need something like two hundred thousand units.

**Bohr** But two hundred million is one thing; two hundred thousand is another. You might just possibly have imagined setting up two hundred thousand.

**Heisenberg** Just possibly.

**Bohr** The Americans did imagine it.

**Heisenberg** Because Otto Frisch and Rudolf Peierls actually did the calculation. They solved the diffusion equation.

**Bohr** Frisch was my old assistant.

**Heisenberg** Peierls was my old pupil.

**Bohr** An Austrian and a German.

**Heisenberg** So they should have been making their calculation for us, at the Kaiser Wilhelm Institute in Berlin. But instead they made it at the University of Birmingham, in England.

**Margrethe** Because they were Jews.

**Heisenberg** There's something almost mathematically elegant about that.

**Bohr** They also started with Perrin and Flügge.

**Heisenberg** They also thought it would take tons. They also thought it was unimaginable.

**Bohr** Until one day . . .

**Heisenberg** They did the calculation.

**Bohr** They discovered just how fast the chain reaction would go.

**Heisenberg**   And therefore how little material you'd need.

**Bohr**   They said slightly over half a kilogram.

**Heisenberg**   About the size of a tennis ball.

**Bohr**   They were wrong, of course.

**Heisenberg**   It was a hundredth of the correct figure.

**Bohr**   Which made it seem a hundred times more imaginable than it actually was.

**Heisenberg**   Whereas I left it seeming twenty times more unimaginable.

**Bohr**   So all your agonising in Copenhagen about plutonium was beside the point. You could have done it without ever building the reactor. You could have done it with 235 all the time.

**Heisenberg**   Almost certainly not.

**Bohr**   Just possibly, though.

**Heisenberg**   Just possibly.

**Bohr**   And *that* question you'd settled long before you arrived in Copenhagen. Simply by failing to try the diffusion equation.

**Heisenberg**   Such a tiny failure.

**Bohr**   But the consequences went branching out over the years, doubling and redoubling.

**Heisenberg**   Until they were large enough to save a city. Which city? Any of the cities that we never dropped our bomb on.

**Bohr**   London, presumably, if you'd had it in time. If the Americans had already entered the war, and the Allies had begun to liberate Europe, then . . .

**Heisenberg**   Who knows? Paris as well. Amsterdam. Perhaps Copenhagen.

**Bohr**    So, Heisenberg, tell us this one simple thing: why didn't you do the calculation?

**Heisenberg**    The question is why Frisch and Peierls *did* do it. It was a stupid waste of time. However much 235 it turned out to be, it was obviously going to be more than anyone could imagine producing.

**Bohr**    Except that it wasn't!

**Heisenberg**    Except that it wasn't.

**Bohr**    So why ... ?

**Heisenberg**    I don't know! I don't know why I didn't do it! Because I never thought of it! Because it didn't occur to me! Because I assumed it wasn't worth doing!

**Bohr**    Assumed? Assumed? You never assumed things! That's how you got uncertainty, because you rejected our assumptions! You calculated, Heisenberg! You calculated everything! The first thing you did with a problem was the mathematics!

**Heisenberg**    You should have been there to slow me down.

**Bohr**    Yes, you wouldn't have got away with it if I'd been standing over you.

**Heisenberg**    Though in fact you made exactly the same assumption! You thought there was no danger for exactly the same reason as I did! Why didn't *you* calculate it?

**Bohr**    Why didn't *I* calculate it?

**Heisenberg**    Tell us why *you* didn't calculate it and we'll know why *I* didn't!

**Bohr**    It's obvious why *I* didn't!

**Heisenberg**    Go on.

**Margrethe**    Because he wasn't trying to build a bomb!

**Heisenberg**    Yes. Thank you. Because he wasn't trying to build a bomb. I imagine it was the same with me. Because

*I* wasn't trying to build a bomb. Thank you.

**Bohr**    So, you bluffed yourself, the way I did at poker with the straight I never had. But in that case . . .

**Heisenberg**    Why did I come to Copenhagen? Yes, why did I come . . . ?

**Bohr**    One more draft, yes? One final draft!

**Heisenberg**    And once again I crunch over the familiar gravel to the Bohrs' front door, and tug at the familiar bell-pull. Why have I come? I know perfectly well. Know so well that I've no need to ask myself. Until once again the heavy front door opens.

**Bohr**    He stands on the doorstep blinking in the sudden flood of light from the house. Until this instant his thoughts have been everywhere and nowhere, like unobserved particles, through all the slits in the diffraction grating simultaneously. Now they have to be observed and specified.

**Heisenberg**    And at once the clear purposes inside my head lose all definite shape. The light falls on them and they scatter.

**Bohr**    My dear Heisenberg!

**Heisenberg**    My dear Bohr!

**Bohr**    Come in, come in . . .

**Heisenberg**    How difficult it is to see even what's in front of one's eyes. All we possess is the present, and the present endlessly dissolves into the past. Bohr has gone even as I turn to see Margrethe.

**Margrethe**    Niels is right. You look older.

**Bohr**    I believe you had some personal trouble.

**Heisenberg**    Margrethe slips into history even as I turn back to Bohr. And yet how much more difficult still it is to catch the slightest glimpse of what's behind one's eyes. Here I am at the centre of the universe, and yet all I can see are two smiles that don't belong to me.

**Margrethe**    How is Elisabeth? How are the children?

**Heisenberg**    Very well. They send their love, of course
... I can feel a third smile in the room, very close to me.
Could it be the one I suddenly see for a moment in the
mirror there? And is the awkward stranger wearing it in
any way connected with this presence that I can feel in the
room? This all-enveloping, unobserved presence?

**Margrethe**    I watch the two smiles in the room, one
awkward and ingratiating, the other rapidly fading from
incautious warmth to bare politeness. There's also a third
smile in the room, I know, unchangingly courteous, I hope,
and unchangingly guarded.

**Heisenberg**    You've managed to get some ski-ing?

**Bohr**    I glance at Margrethe, and for a moment I see
what she can see and I can't – myself, and the smile
vanishing from my face as poor Heisenberg blunders on.

**Heisenberg**    I look at the two of them looking at me,
and for a moment I see the third person in the room as
clearly as I see them. Their importunate guest, stumbling
from one crass and unwelcome thoughtfulness to the next.

**Bohr**    I look at him looking at me, anxiously, pleadingly,
urging me back to the old days, and I see what he sees.
And yes – now it comes, now it comes – there's someone
missing from the room. He sees me. He sees Margrethe.
He doesn't see himself.

**Heisenberg**    Two thousand million people in the world,
and the one who has to decide their fate is the only one
who's always hidden from me.

**Bohr**    You suggested a stroll.

**Heisenberg**    You remember Elsinore? The darkness
inside the human soul . . . ?

**Bohr**    And out we go. Out under the autumn trees.

Through the blacked-out streets.

**Heisenberg**   Now there's no one in the world except Bohr and the invisible other. Who is he, this all-enveloping presence in the darkness?

**Margrethe**   The flying particle wanders the darkness, no one knows where. It's here, it's there, it's everywhere and nowhere.

**Bohr**   With careful casualness he begins to ask the question he's prepared.

**Heisenberg**   Does one as a physicist have the moral right to work on the practical exploitation of atomic energy?

**Margrethe**   The great collision.

**Bohr**   I stop. He stops . . .

**Margrethe**   This is how they work.

**Heisenberg**   He gazes at me, horrified.

**Margrethe**   Now at last he knows where he is and what he's doing.

**Heisenberg**   He turns away.

**Margrethe**   And even as the moment of collision begins it's over.

**Bohr**   Already we're hurrying back towards the house.

**Margrethe**   Already they're both flying away from each other into the darkness again.

**Heisenberg**   Our conversation's over.

**Bohr**   Our great partnership.

**Heisenberg**   All our friendship.

**Margrethe**   And everything about him becomes as uncertain as it was before.

**Bohr**   Unless . . . yes . . . a thought-experiment. . . . Let's suppose for a moment that I don't go flying off into the night. Let's see what happens if instead I remember the paternal role I'm supposed to play. If I stop, and control my anger, and turn to him. And ask him why.

**Heisenberg**  Why?

**Bohr**  Why are you confident that it's going to be so reassuringly difficult to build a bomb with 235? Is it because you've done the calculation?

**Heisenberg**  The calculation?

**Bohr**  Of the diffusion in 235. No. It's because you haven't calculated it. You haven't considered calculating it. You hadn't consciously realised there was a calculation to be made.

**Heisenberg**  And of course now I *have* realised. In fact it wouldn't be all that difficult. Let's see. . . . The scattering cross-section's about $6 \times 10^{-24}$, so the mean free path would be . . . Hold on . . .

**Bohr**  And suddenly a very different and very terrible new world begins to take shape . . .

**Margrethe**  That was the last and greatest demand that Heisenberg made on his friendship with you. To be understood when he couldn't understand himself. And that was the last and greatest act of friendship for Heisenberg that you performed in return. To leave him misunderstood.

**Heisenberg**  Yes. Perhaps I should thank you.

**Bohr**  Perhaps you should.

**Margrethe**  Anyway, it was the end of the story.

**Bohr**  Though perhaps there was also something I should thank *you* for. That summer night in 1943, when I escaped across the Sound in the fishing-boat, and the freighters arrived from Germany . . .

**Margrethe**  What's that to do with Heisenberg?

**Bohr**  When the ships arrived on the Wednesday there were eight thousand Jews in Denmark to be arrested and crammed into their holds. On the Friday evening, at the start of the Sabbath, when the SS began their round-up, there was scarcely a Jew to be found.

**Margrethe**    They'd all been hidden in churches and hospitals, in people's homes and country cottages.

**Bohr**    But how was that possible? – Because we'd been tipped off by someone in the German Embassy.

**Heisenberg**    Georg Duckwitz, their shipping specialist.

**Bohr**    Your man?

**Heisenberg**    One of them.

**Bohr**    He was a remarkable informant. He told us the day before the freighters arrived – the very day that Hitler issued the order. He gave us the exact time that the SS would move.

**Margrethe**    It was the Resistance who got them out of their hiding-places and smuggled them across the Sound.

**Bohr**    For a handful of us in one fishing smack to get past the German patrol-boats was remarkable enough. For a whole armada to get past, with the best part of eight thousand people on board, was like the Red Sea parting.

**Margrethe**    I thought there *were* no German patrol-boats that night?

**Bohr**    No – the whole squadron had suddenly been reported unseaworthy.

**Heisenberg**    How they got away with it I can't imagine.

**Bohr**    Duckwitz again?

**Heisenberg**    He also went to Stockholm and asked the Swedish Government to accept everyone.

**Bohr**    So perhaps I should thank you.

**Heisenberg**    For what?

**Bohr**    My life. All our lives.

**Heisenberg**  Nothing to do with me by that time. I regret to say.

**Bohr**  But after I'd gone you came back to Copenhagen.

**Heisenberg**  To make sure that our people didn't take over the Institute in your absence.

**Bohr**  I've never thanked you for that, either.

**Heisenberg**  You know they offered me your cyclotron?

**Bohr**  You could have separated a little 235 with it.

**Heisenberg**  Meanwhile you were going on from Sweden to Los Alamos.

**Bohr**  To play my small but helpful part in the deaths of a hundred thousand people.

**Margrethe**  Niels, you did nothing wrong!

**Bohr**  Didn't I?

**Heisenberg**  Of course not. You were a good man, from first to last, and no one could ever say otherwise. Whereas I . . .

**Bohr**  Whereas you, my dear Heisenberg, never managed to contribute to the death of one single solitary person in all your life.

**Margrethe**  Well, yes.

**Heisenberg**  Did I?

**Margrethe**  One. Or so you told us. The poor fellow you guarded overnight, when you were a boy in Munich, while he was waiting to be shot in the morning.

**Bohr**  All right then, one. One single soul on his conscience, to set against all the others.

**Margrethe**  But that one single soul was emperor of the universe, no less than each of us. Until the morning came.

**Heisenberg**  No, when the morning came I persuaded them to let him go.

**Bohr**   Heisenberg, I have to say – if people are to be measured strictly in terms of observable quantities . . .

**Heisenberg**   Then we should need a strange new quantum ethics. There'd be a place in heaven for me. And another one for the SS man I met on my way home from Haigerloch. That was the end of my war. The Allied troops were closing in; there was nothing more we could do. Elisabeth and the children had taken refuge in a village in Bavaria, so I went to see them before I was captured. I had to go by bicycle – there were no trains or road transport by that time – and I had to travel by night and sleep under a hedge by day, because all through the daylight hours the skies were full of Allied planes, scouring the roads for anything that moved. A man on a bicycle would have been the biggest target left in Germany. Three days and three nights I travelled. Out of Württemberg, down through the Swabian Jura and the first foothills of the Alps. Across my ruined homeland. Was this what I'd chosen for it? This endless rubble? This perpetual smoke in the sky? These hungry faces? Was this my doing? And all the desperate people on the roads. The most desperate of all were the SS. Bands of fanatics with nothing left to lose, roaming around shooting deserters out of hand, hanging them from roadside trees. The second night, and suddenly there it is – the terrible familiar black tunic emerging from the twilight in front of me. On his lips as I stop – the one terrible familiar word. 'Deserter,' he says. He sounds as exhausted as I am. I give him the travel order I've written for myself. But there's hardly enough light in the sky to read by, and he's too weary to bother. He begins to open his holster instead. He's going to shoot me because it's simply less labour. And suddenly I'm thinking very quickly and clearly – it's like ski-ing, or that night on Heligoland, or the one in Faelled Park. What comes into my mind this time is the pack of American cigarettes I've got in my pocket. And already it's in my hand – I'm holding it out to him. The most desperate solution to a problem yet. I wait while he stands there looking at it, trying to make it out, trying to think, his left hand holding my useless piece of paper, his right on the fastening of the holster. There are two simple words in large print on the pack: Lucky Strike. He closes the holster, and takes the cigarettes instead. . . . It had worked, it had worked! Like all the other solutions to all the other problems. For twenty cigarettes he let me live. And on I went. Three days and three nights. Past the weeping children, the lost and hungry children, drafted to fight, then abandoned by their commanders. Past the starving slave-labourers walking home to France, to Poland, to Estonia. Through Gammertingen and Biberach and Memmingen. Mindelheim, Kaufbeuren, and Schöngau. Across my beloved homeland. My ruined and dishonoured and beloved homeland.

**Bohr**   My dear Heisenberg! My dear friend!

**Margrethe**   Silence. The silence we always in the end return to.

**Heisenberg**   And of course I know what they're thinking about.

**Margrethe**   All those lost children on the road.

**Bohr**   Heisenberg wandering the world like a lost child himself.

**Margrethe**   Our own lost children.

**Heisenberg**   And over goes the tiller once again.

**Bohr**   So near, so near! So slight a thing!

**Margrethe**   He stands in the doorway, watching me, then he turns his head away . . .

**Heisenberg**   And once again away he goes, into the dark waters.

**Bohr**   Before we can lay our hands on anything, our life's over.

**Heisenberg**   Before we can glimpse who or what we are, we're gone and laid to dust.

**Bohr**   Settled among all the dust we raised.

**Margrethe**   And sooner or later there will come a time when all our children are laid to dust, and all our children's children.

**Bohr**   When no more decisions, great or small, are ever made again. When there's no more uncertainty, because there's no more knowledge.

**Margrethe**   And when all our eyes are closed, when even the ghosts have gone, what will be left of our beloved world? Our ruined and dishonoured and beloved world?

**Heisenberg**   But in the meanwhile, in this most precious meanwhile, there it is. The trees in Faelled Park. Gammertingen and Biberach and Mindelheim. Our children and our children's children. Preserved, just possibly, by that one short moment in Copenhagen. By some event that will never quite be located or defined. By that final core of uncertainty at the heart of things.

# POSTSCRIPT

Where a work of fiction features historical characters and historical events it's reasonable to want to know how much of it is fiction and how much of it is history. So let me make it as clear as I can in regard to this play.

The central event in it is a real one. Heisenberg *did* go to Copenhagen in 1941, and there *was* a meeting with Bohr, in the teeth of all the difficulties encountered by my characters. He probably went to dinner at the Bohrs' house, and the two men probably went for a walk to escape from any possible microphones, though there is some dispute about even these simple matters. The question of what they actually said to each other has been even more disputed, and where there's ambiguity in the play about what happened, it's because there is in the recollection of the participants. Much more sustained speculation still has been devoted to the question of what Heisenberg was hoping to achieve by the meeting. All the alternative and co-existing explications offered in the play, except perhaps the final one, have been aired at various times, in one form or another.

Most anxious of all to establish some agreed version of the meeting was Heisenberg himself. He did indeed go back in 1947 with his British minder, Ronald Fraser, and attempted to find some common ground in the matter with Bohr. But it proved to be too delicate a task, and (according to Heisenberg, at any rate, in his memoirs) 'we both came to feel that it would be better to stop disturbing the spirits of the past.' This is where my play departs from the historical record, by supposing that at some later time, when everyone involved had become spirits of the past themselves, they argued the question out further, until they had achieved a little more understanding of what was going on, just as they had so many times when they were alive with the intractable difficulties presented by the internal workings of the atom.

The account of these earlier discussions in the twenties reflects at any rate one or two of the key topics, and the passion with which the argument was conducted, as it emerges from the biographical and autobiographical record.

I am acutely aware of how over-simplified my version is.
Max Born described the real story as not so much 'a straight
staircase upwards, but a tangle of interconnected alleys', and
I have found it impossible to follow these in any detail (even
where I can begin to understand them). In particular I have
grossly understated the crucial role played by Born himself
and by his pupil Pascual Jordan at Göttingen in formulating
quantum mechanics (it was Born who supplied the
understanding of matrices that Heisenberg lacked, and the
statistical interpretation of Schrödinger's wave function), and
of Wolfgang Pauli in Hamburg, whose exclusion principle
filled in one of the key pieces in the puzzle.

But the account of the German and American bomb
programmes, and of the two physicists' participation in them,
is taken from the historical record; so is the fate of Danish
Jewry; Heisenberg's experiences in Germany before and
during the war, his subsequent internment, and the
depression that clouded his later years. I have filled out some
of the details, but in general what he says happened to him
– at the end of the First World War, on Heligoland, during
his nocturnal walk in Faelled Park, during the Berlin air-raid
and his internment, and on his ride across Germany, with its
near-fatal encounter along the way – is based very closely
upon the accounts he gave in life.

The actual words spoken by my characters are of course
entirely their own. If this needs any justification then I can
only appeal to Heisenberg himself. In his memoirs dialogue
plays an important part, he says, because he hopes 'to
demonstrate that science is rooted in conversations'. But, as
he explains, conversations, even real conversations, cannot be
reconstructed literally several decades later. So he freely
reinvents them, and appeals in his turn to Thucydides.
(Heisenberg's father was a professor of classics, and he was
an accomplished classicist himself, on top of all his other
distinctions.) Thucydides explains in his preface to the *History
of the Peloponnesian War* that, although he had avoided all
'storytelling', when it came to the speeches, 'I have found it
impossible to remember their exact wording. Hence I have
made each orator speak as, in my opinion, he would have

done in the circumstances, but keeping as close as I could to the train of thought that guided his actual speech.'
Thucydides was trying to give an account of speeches that had actually been made, many of which he had himself heard. Some of the dialogue in my play represents speeches that must have been made in one form or another; some of it speeches that were certainly never made at all. I hope, though, that in some sense it respects the Thucydidean principle, and that speeches (and indeed actions) follow in so far as possible the original protagonists' train of thought.

But how far is it possible to know what their train of thought was? This is where I have departed from the established historical record – from any possible historical record. The great challenge facing the storyteller and the historian alike is to get inside people's heads, to stand where they stood and see the world as they saw it, to make some informed estimate of their motives and intentions – and this is precisely where recorded and recordable history cannot reach. Even when all the external evidence has been mastered, the only way into the protagonists' heads is through the imagination. This indeed is the substance of the play.

*

I can't claim to be the first person to notice the parallels between Heisenberg's science and his life. They provide David Cassidy with the title (*Uncertainty*) for his excellent biography (the standard work in English). 'Especially difficult and controversial,' says Cassidy in his introduction, 'is a retrospective evaluation of Heisenberg's activities during the Third Reich and particularly during World War II. Since the end of the war, an enormous range of views about this man and his behaviour have been expressed, views that have been fervently, even passionately, held by a variety of individuals. It is as if, for some, the intense emotions unleashed by the unspeakable horrors of that war and regime have combined with the many ambiguities, dualities, and compromises of Heisenberg's life and actions to make

Heisenberg himself subject to a type of uncertainty principle
. . .' Thomas Powers makes a similar point in his
extraordinary and encyclopaedic book *Heisenberg's War*, which
first aroused my interest in the trip to Copenhagen; he says
that Heisenberg's later reticence on his role in the failure of
the German bomb programme 'introduces an element of
irreducible uncertainty'.

Cassidy does not explore the parallel further. Powers even
appends a footnote to his comment: 'Forgive me.' The
apology seems to me unnecessary. It's true that the concept
of uncertainty is one of those scientific notions that has
become common coinage, and generalised to the point of
losing much of its original meaning. The idea as introduced
by Heisenberg into quantum mechanics was precise and
technical. It didn't suggest that everything about the
behaviour of particles was unknowable, or hazy. What it
limited was the simultaneous measurement of 'canonically
conjugate variables', such as position and momentum, or
energy and time. The more precisely you measure one
variable, it said, the less precise your measurement of the
related variable can be; and this ratio, the uncertainty
relationship, is itself precisely formulable.

None of this, plainly, applies directly to our observations
of thought and intention. Thoughts are not locatable by pairs
of conjugate variables, so there can be no question of a ratio
of precision. Powers seems to imply that in Heisenberg's case
the uncertainty arises purely because 'questions of motive
and intention cannot be established more clearly than he was
willing to state them'. It's true that Heisenberg was under
contradictory pressures after the war which made it
particularly difficult for him to explain what he had been
trying to do. He wanted to distance himself from the Nazis,
but he didn't want to suggest that he had been a traitor. He
was reluctant to claim to his fellow-Germans that he had
deliberately lost them the war, but he was no less reluctant
to suggest that he had failed them simply out of
incompetence.

But the uncertainty surely begins long before the point
where Heisenberg might have offered an explanation. He

was under at least as many contradictory pressures at the time to shape the actions he later failed to explain, and the uncertainty would still have existed, for us and for him, even if he had been as open, honest, and helpful as it is humanly possible to be. What people say about their own motives and intentions, even when they are not caught in the traps that entangled Heisenberg, is always subject to question – as subject to question as what anybody else says about them. Thoughts and intentions, even one's own – perhaps one's own most of all – remain shifting and elusive. There is not one single thought or intention of any sort that can ever be precisely established.

What the uncertainty of thoughts does have in common with the uncertainty of particles is that the difficulty is not just a practical one, but a systematic limitation which cannot even in theory be circumvented. It is patently not resolved by the efforts of psychologists and psycho-analysts, and it will not be resolved by neurologists, either, even when everything is known about the structure and workings of the brain, any more than semantic questions can be resolved by looking at the machine code of a computer. And since, according to the so-called 'Copenhagen Interpretation' of quantum mechanics – the interconnected set of theories that was developed by Heisenberg, Bohr, and others in the twenties – the whole possibility of saying or thinking anything about the world, even the most apparently objective, abstract aspects of it studied by the natural sciences, depends upon human observation, and is subject to the limitations which the human mind imposes, this uncertainty in our thinking is also fundamental to the nature of the world.

'Uncertainty' is not a very satisfactory word to come at this. It sits awkwardly even in its original context. You can be uncertain about things which are themselves entirely definite, and about which you could be entirely certain if you were simply better informed. Indeed, the very idea of uncertainty seems to imply the possibility of certainty. Heisenberg and Bohr used several different German words in different contexts. Bohr (who spoke more or less perfect

German) sometimes referred to *Unsicherheit,* which means quite simply unsureness. In Heisenberg's original paper he talks about *Ungenauigkeit* – inexactness – and the most usual term now in German seems to be *Unschärfe* – blurredness or fuzziness. But the word he adopts in his general conclusion, and which he uses when he refers back to the period later in his memoirs, is *Unbestimmtheit,* for which it's harder to find a satisfactory English equivalent. Although it means uncertainty in the sense of vagueness, it's plainly derived from *bestimmen,* to determine or to ascertain. This is reflected better in the other English translation which is sometimes used, but which seems to be less familiar: indeterminacy. 'Undeterminedness' would be closer still, though clumsy. Less close to the German, but even closer to the reality of the situation, would be 'indeterminability'.

Questions of translation apart, Heisenberg's choice of word suggests that, at the time he wrote his paper, he had not fully grasped the metaphysical implications of what he was saying. Indeed, he concludes that the experiments concerned are affected by *Unbestimmtheit* 'purely empirically'. He was not, as Bohr complained, at that time greatly interested in the philosophical fallout from physics and mathematics (though he became much more so later on in life), and he was publishing in a hurry, as Bohr also complained, before he had had a chance to discuss the work with either Bohr or anyone else. His paper seems to imply that electrons have definite orbits, even if these are unknowable; he talks about a quantum of light completely throwing the electron out of its 'orbit', even though he puts the word into inverted commas, and says that it has no rational sense here. The title of the paper itself reinforces this impression: *Über den anschaulichen Inhalt der quantentheoretischen Kinematik und Mechanik.* Again there are translation problems. '*Anschaulich*' means graphic, concrete, 'look-at-able'; the title is usually translated as referring to the 'perceptual' content of the disciplines concerned, which again seems to suggest a contrast with their unperceived aspects – as if Heisenberg were concerned merely about our difficulties in visualising abstractions, not about the physical implications of this.

*

The Copenhagen Interpretation of quantum mechanics was
scientific orthodoxy for most of the twentieth century, and is
the theoretical basis (for better or worse) on which the
century's dramatic physical demonstrations of nuclear forces
were constructed. But it has not gone unchallenged. Einstein
never accepted it, though he could never find a way round
it. The mathematician Roger Penrose regards the present
state of quantum theory as 'provisional', and quotes
Schrödinger, de Broglie, and Dirac as forerunners in this
view.

An alternative to the Copenhagen Interpretation,
explaining the apparent superimposition of different states
that appears at the quantum level in terms of a multiplicity
of parallel worlds, was developed after the Second World
War by Hugh Everett III, who had been a graduate student
of John Wheeler, Bohr's associate in the famous paper which
opened the way to an understanding of uranium fission.
David Deutsch, who proposes an extreme version of
Everett's ideas in his book *The Fabric of Reality*, claims that
'hardly anyone' still believes in the Copenhagen
Interpretation. I have put this view to a number of physicists.
They all seemed greatly surprised by it; but maybe I have
hit upon precisely the supposed handful who remain in the
faith.

Another follower of Everett (though he seems to differ
quite sharply from Deutsch) is Murray Gell-Mann, who with
Yuval Ne'eman revolutionised elementary particle theory in
the sixties with the introduction of the quark, in its three
different 'colours' and six different 'flavours', as the
fundamental unit of the material world. Gell-Mann believes
that quantum mechanics is the fundamental tool for
understanding the universe, but he sees the Copenhagen
Interpretation, with its dependence upon an observer and the
human act of measurement, as anthropocentric, and as
characterising merely a special case that he calls 'the
approximate quantum mechanics of measured systems'. I
hesitate to express any reservations about something I

understand so little, particularly when it comes from such an authority, but it seems to me that the view which Gell-Mann favours, and which involves what he calls alternative 'histories' or 'narratives', is precisely as anthropocentric as Bohr's, since histories and narratives are not freestanding elements of the universe, but human constructs as subjective and as restricted in their viewpoint as the act of observation.

The relevance of indeterminacy to quantum mechanics has also been challenged. A version of the famous thought experiment involving two slits has now actually been carried out in the laboratory (at the University of Konstanz). It confirms, as Bohr hypothesised, that while an unobserved particle seems to pass through both slits, so that it forms a characteristic interference pattern on a screen beyond them, any act of observation that attempts to determine which of the two paths the particle actually follows necessarily destroys the phenomenon, so that the interference pattern vanishes. But the experiment appears to suggest that, although the uncertainty principle is true, it accounts for discrepancies far too small to explain the loss of interference. The observation in the laboratory experiment, moreover, was carried out not, as in the old thought experiment, by hitting the particle involved with a photon, which transfers part of its energy to the particle and so alters its path, but by a way of marking with microwaves which has almost no effect on the particle's momentum.

Some physicists now accept that the loss of interference is caused by a much stranger and less quasi-classical aspect of the quantum world – entanglement. The notion was introduced by Schrödinger in 1935, and suggests that where quantum-mechanical entities become involved with each other (as with the particle and the photon), they form states of affairs which continue to have a collective identity and behaviour, even though their components have physically separated again. The difficulties in this are obvious, but there is no interpretation of quantum-mechanical phenomena that does not involve breathtaking challenges to the logic of our everyday experience.

For the references to all these developments see the

bibliography at the end of this Postscript.

\*

What about my characters? Are they anything like their originals?

It's impossible to catch the exact tone of voice of people one never knew, with only the written record to go on, especially when most of what their contemporaries recall them as saying was originally said in other languages. There are also more particular problems with all three of my protagonists.

Bohr, for a start, was as notorious for his inarticulacy and inaudibility as he was famous for his goodness and lovability. He was fluent in various languages, but I have heard it said that the problem was to know which language he was being fluent in. Schrödinger, after his epic confrontation with Bohr in 1926, described him as often talking 'for minutes almost in a dreamlike, visionary and really quite unclear manner, partly because he is so full of consideration and constantly hesitates – fearing that the other might take a statement of his [Bohr's] point of view as an insufficient appreciation of the other's . . .' My Bohr is necessarily a little more coherent than this – and I have been told by various correspondents who knew him that in private, if not in public, he could be much more cogent and incisive than Schrödinger evidently found him.

The problem with Margrethe is that there is relatively little biographical material to go on. She and Niels were plainly mutually devoted, and everything suggests that she was as generally loved as he was. She had no scientific training, but Bohr constantly discussed his work with her, presumably avoiding technical language – though she must have become fairly familiar with even that since she typed out each draft of his papers. I suspect she was more gracious and reserved than she appears here, but she plainly had great firmness of character – in later life she was known as *Dronning* (Queen) Margrethe. She was always cooler about Heisenberg than Bohr was, and she was openly angry about his visit in 1941. According to Bohr she objected strongly to his being invited to the house, and relented only when Bohr promised to avoid politics and restrict the conversation to physics. Bohr himself always refused to be drawn about Heisenberg's trip in 1941, but she insisted, even after the war, even after all Heisenberg's attempts to explain, 'No matter what anyone says, that was a hostile visit.'

The problem with Heisenberg is his elusiveness and ambiguity, which is of course what the play is attempting to elucidate. The one thing about him that everyone agreed upon was what Max Born, his mentor in Göttingen, called 'his unbelievable quickness and precision of understanding'. The contrast with Bohr is almost comic. 'Probably [Bohr's] most characteristic property,' according to George Gamow, 'was the slowness of his thinking and comprehension.'

As a young man Heisenberg seems to have had an appealing eagerness and directness. Born described him as looking like a simple farm boy, with clear bright eyes, and a radiant expression on his face. Somebody else thought he looked 'like a bright carpenter's apprentice just returned from technical school'. Victor Weisskopf says that he made friends easily, and that everyone liked him. Bohr, after their first meeting in 1922, was delighted by Heisenberg's 'nice shy nature, his good temper, his eagerness and his enthusiasm'. There was something about him of the prize-winning student, who is good at everything required of him, and Bohr was not the only father-figure to whom he appealed. He had a somewhat similar relationship to Sommerfeld, his first professor in Munich, and in his difficulties with the Nazis he turned to two elders of German physics for counsel, Max Planck and Max von Laue. His closest friend and colleague was probably Carl Friedrich von Weizsäcker, who was younger than him, but it is striking that during his internment the person he chose to confide his explanation of the Hiroshima bomb to was not Weizsäcker, who was interned with him (although he may well have discussed it with him already), but the 66-year-old Otto Hahn.

The American physicist Jeremy Bernstein says that 'he

had the first truly quantum-mechanical mind – the ability to take the leap beyond the classical visualising pictures into the abstract, all-but-impossible-to-visualise world of the subatomic . . .' Cassidy believes that a great part of his genius was his 'ability to adopt a serviceable solution regardless of accepted wisdom'. Rudolf Peierls stresses his intuition. He would 'almost always intuitively know the answer to a problem, then look for a mathematical solution to give it to him'. The obverse of this, according to Peierls, is that 'he was always very casual about numbers' – a weakness that seems to have contributed to his downfall – or his salvation – in the atomic bomb programme.

Margrethe always found him difficult, closed, and oversensitive, and this propensity to be withdrawn and inturned was exacerbated as life went on – first by his political problems in the thirties, and then by his efforts to reconcile the moral irreconcilables of his wartime work. His autobiographical writing is rather stiff and formal, and his letters to Bohr, even during the twenties and thirties, are correct rather than intimate. Throughout the period of their closest friendship they addressed each other with the formal *Sie*, and switched to *Du* only when Heisenberg also had a chair.

The conversations that Heisenberg claimed such freedom to recreate in his memoirs are stately. Much more plausibly colloquial is the transcript of David Irving's long interview with him for *The Virus House*, Irving's history of the German bomb programme, though he is still (naturally) watchful. In the transcripts of the relatively unguarded conversations that the German atomic team had among themselves during their internment, where Heisenberg emerges as the dominant figure, both morally and practically, a certain hard-headed worldliness can be detected. He is much concerned with professional prospects, and with how they might make some money out of their wartime researches. When one of the others says that if they agree to work on atomic matters under Allied control they will be looked down upon as traitors 'in the eyes of the masses', Heisenberg replies: 'No. One must do that cleverly. As far as the masses are concerned it will look as though we unfortunately have to continue our scientific work under the wicked Anglo-Saxon control, and that we can do nothing about it. We will have to appear to accept this control with fury and gnashing of teeth.'

There was always something a little sharp and harsh about him, something that at its best inspired respect rather than love, and that after the war occasioned really quite astonishing hostility and contempt. Even Samuel Goudsmit turned against him. Goudsmit was an old friend and colleague; when the investigators of the Alsos mission, the Allied agency for gathering intelligence on German atomic research, for which he was working, finally broke into Heisenberg's office in 1945, one of the first things they saw was a picture of the two of them together that Heisenberg had kept there as a memento of happier days. But when Goudsmit subsequently interrogated Heisenberg he found him arrogant and self-involved. Goudsmit had understandably bitter feelings at the time – he had just discovered the record of his parents' death in Auschwitz. Heisenberg was also caught in a false position. Confident that his team had been far ahead of the Americans, he offered Goudsmit his services in initiating them into the secrets of uranium fission. (Goudsmit did nothing to correct his misapprehension, which gave Heisenberg, when the truth finally came out, grounds for returning Goudsmit's bitterness.) In his superficial and strangely unimpressive book on Alsos, Goudsmit wrote about Heisenberg and his team with contemptuous dismissal, and in the year-long correspondence in the American press that followed its publication, accused him of self-importance and dishonesty.

Weisskopf gave a reception for Heisenberg during his trip to America in 1949, but about half the guests – including many people from the Los Alamos team – failed to appear, explaining to Weisskopf that they didn't want to shake the hand of the man who had tried to build a bomb for Hitler. Even Cassidy, who gives full measure to Heisenberg as a physicist in his biography, is notably cool and cautious in his assessment of Heisenberg's role in the German bomb

programme. Ronald Fraser, the British intelligence officer
who escorted Heisenberg back to Copenhagen in 1947 (the
British seem to have been frightened that he would defect to
the Russians, or be kidnapped by them) replied to Irving's
inquiry about the trip in tones of patronising contempt that
seem slightly unhinged. 'The whole story of "a kind of
confrontation",' he wrote to Irving, 'in the matter of his
1941 natter with Bohr in the Tivoli Gardens [sic] is a typical
Heisenberg fabrication – maybe a bit brighter than a
thousand others, but like them all a product of his *Blut und
Boden* guilt complex, which he rationalises that quickly that
the stories become *for him* the truth, the whole truth, and
nothing but the truth. Pitiful, in a man of his mental stature.'

The historian Paul Lawrence Rose, who has focused
upon Heisenberg as an emblem for what he regards as the
general failings of German culture, also takes a remarkably
high moral tone. In a paper he wrote in 1984, entitled
*Heisenberg, German Morality and the Atomic Bomb,* he talked about
Heisenberg's 'guff', his 'self-serving, self-deluding claims',
and his 'elementary moral stupidity'. After a further fourteen
years research Professor Rose returned to the subject in 1998
in a full-length book which was published after the play was
produced, and which has attracted considerable attention,
*Heisenberg and the Nazi Atomic Bomb Project: a Study in German
Culture.* His contempt for Heisenberg remains unmoderated.
He believes that Heisenberg failed, in spite of his perfect
readiness to serve the Nazi regime, because of his arrogance
and wrong-headedness, and because he embodied various
vices of German culture in general, and of the Nazi regime
in particular, whose values he had absorbed.

It is a difficult book to read – Rose can scarcely quote a
word of Heisenberg's without adding his own disparaging
qualification. Here is a selection of his interjections on two
facing pages taken more or less at random: ' . . . self-
incriminating . . . a somewhat inadequate explanation . . .
this inconsistency . . . the falseness of these lame excuses . . .
a characteristic Heisenberg lie . . . Heisenberg's usual facile
rationalising ability . . . Heisenberg then went on glibly to

recollect . . . the delusory nature of Heisenberg's
memory . . .'

You wonder at times whether it wouldn't look better if it
were handwritten in green ink, with no paragraph breaks.
Rose seems to be aware himself of the effect he is producing.
He realises, he says, that some readers may 'find distasteful
the recurrent moral judgments passed on Heisenberg'. They
may also, he thinks, be put off by what seems a 'lack of
sympathy with German culture' – he cannot say, he
confesses, that his 'British background' has made him
entirely sympathetic to it. He is at pains to distance himself
from any unfortunate echoes that this attitude may awaken:
he hopes that readers will not accuse him of 'unthinkingly
preaching a crude view of German "national character",
whatever that term may mean'. What he is concerned with,
he explains, is not that at all, but 'the enduring nature of
what one might call the "deep culture" of Germany . . . In
this book I have tried to penetrate into how Germans think
– or rather, perhaps, used to think – and to show how
radically different are German and what I have termed
"Western" mentalities and sensibilities.' It is this that
underlies what he calls, without apparent irony, 'the
Heisenberg problem'.

Some of his evidence induces a certain dizziness. He
quotes without comment, as the epigraph to a chapter, a
remark by Albert Speer, the Nazi Minister of Armaments: 'I
do hope Heisenberg is not now claiming that they tried, for
reasons of principle, to sabotage the project by asking for
such minimal support!' It's true that any claim to have
sabotaged the project, particularly for reasons of principle,
would represent an astonishing departure from Heisenberg's
habitual caution on the subject. But the question is not what
Speer hoped, but whether Heisenberg *did* make such a claim.

So did he or didn't he? Rose doesn't tell us, and the only
reference he gives is Gitta Sereny's new book, *Albert Speer: His
Battle with Truth*. The allusion is to the crucial meeting at
Harnack House in 1942, mentioned in the play. Speer said
in his memoirs that he was 'rather put out' by the very small
amount of money that Heisenberg requested to run the
nuclear research programme. In an earlier draft of the

manuscript (the 'Spandau draft'), says Sereny, he had added in brackets the remark that Rose quotes – and Heisenberg, she says, 'did in fact try precisely that after the war'.

So he *did* make the claim! But when and where? Sereny doesn't tell us. The only references to the smallness of the sums of money he asked for that I can find in the record are the one quoted, by Speer himself, and another by Field Marshal Milch, Goering's deputy in the Luftwaffe, who was also present at the meeting. There's certainly nothing about it in Heisenberg's memoirs, or in Robert Jungk's book, *Brighter Than a Thousand Suns*, or in Heisenberg's long interview with Irving, or in the other two obvious places, his interview with *Der Spiegel* in 1967, when Irving's book was published, or his review of the book in the *Frankfurter Allgemeine Zeitung*. I hardly like to put myself forward to fill the gap, but so far as I know the only reference he made to the subject was posthumously and fictitiously in my play.

Sereny, like Rose, is markedly unenthusiastic about Heisenberg in general. She goes on to argue that Heisenberg's claims about his intentions in meeting Bohr in 1941 'are now shown by Speer's Spandau account to be false', though quite how this is so she doesn't explain. About what she calls 'the facts' of the Copenhagen meeting she is remarkably brisk. In the conversation '. . . which Bohr subsequently reported to his associates at the Niels Bohr Institute, Heisenberg had made his political stand crystal clear. His team, he told Bohr, had gone some way towards discovering a way to produce an atom bomb. Germany was going to win the war, probably quite soon, and Bohr should join them now in their efforts.'

The idea that Heisenberg was inviting Bohr to work on the German bomb is on the face of it the least plausible out of all the possible interpretations that have been offered. It is completely at odds with what Weisskopf recalls Bohr as saying in 1948, and with what Bohr is on record as telling Chadwick at the time. In any case, the suggestion that Heisenberg thought he might be able to import someone half-Jewish into the most secret research programme in Nazi Germany is frankly preposterous.

So what is Sereny's evidence for her account of the
meeting? At this point the sense of vertigo returns, and one
begins to have the feeling that one is in an Escher drawing,
where the stairs up to the floor above somehow lead back to
the floor one is already on, because the only reference she
gives is ... Powers, Heisenberg's great champion, in
*Heisenberg's War*.

And it's true – Powers *does* quote an opinion to this effect
(and it's the only possible source for it anywhere, so far as I
know). He says he was told by Weizsäcker that some person
or persons unnamed in Copenhagen, 44 years after the
event, had told *him* that this is what Bohr had said he had
believed Heisenberg's intention to be. One might think that
this is rather faint evidence. In any case, even if it really is
what Bohr believed, it is of course not what Weizsäcker
believed, or Powers either. They are reporting Bohr's alleged
belief as a possible misapprehension on his part which might
have explained his anger. Indeed, Powers's own reading of
the situation is precisely the one that Sereny claims to be
discredited by Speer's remark.

*

Goudsmit gradually modified his opinion, and his final
judgment on Heisenberg, when he died in 1976, was a
generous one which goes some way to expunging the
dismissive tone of his book: 'Heisenberg was a very great
physicist, a deep thinker, a fine human being, and also a
courageous person. He was one of the greatest physicists of
our time, but he suffered severely under the unwarranted
attacks by fanatical colleagues. In my opinion he must be
considered to have been in some respects a victim of the
Nazi regime.'

Robert Jungk, one of the few authors who have ever
attempted to defend Heisenberg, modified his opinion in the
opposite direction. In *Brighter Than a Thousand Suns*, originally
published in 1956, he suggested that the German physicists
had managed to avoid building nuclear weapons for
conscientious reasons, and quoted Heisenberg as saying that,

'under a dictatorship active resistance can only be practised by those who pretend to collaborate with the regime. Anyone speaking out openly against the system thereby indubitably deprives himself of any chance of active resistance.' But Jungk later changed his mind, and described the notion of passive resistance on the part of the German physicists as a 'myth'. He had contributed to spreading it, he said, out of an 'esteem for those impressive personalities which I have since realized to be out of place'.

For a really spirited and sustained defence Heisenberg had to wait until Powers published his book in 1993. It is a remarkable piece of work, journalistic in tone, but generous in its understanding and huge in its scope. A little too huge, perhaps, because Powers is unable to resist being side-tracked from the main narrative by the amazing byways that he perpetually finds opening off it. I recommend it particularly to other dramatists and screenwriters; there is material here for several more plays and films yet.

His central argument is that the Allied bomb programme succeeded because of the uninhibited eagerness of the scientists to do it, particularly of those exiles who had known Nazism at first hand, and who were desperate to pre-empt Hitler; while the German programme failed because of the underlying reluctance of scientists in Germany to arm Hitler with the bomb, however strong their patriotism, and however much they wanted to profit from the possibilities for research. 'Zeal was needed,' he says; 'its absence was lethal, like a poison that leaves no trace.'

But he goes further, and argues that Heisenberg 'did not simply withhold himself, stand aside, let the project die. He killed it.' He tries to show that at every point Heisenberg was careful to hold out enough hope to the authorities to ensure that he and his team were left in charge of the project, but never enough to attract the total commitment and huge investment that would have offered the only real hope of success. 'Heisenberg's caution saved him. He was free to do what he could to guide the German atomic research effort into a broom closet, where scientists tinkered until the war ended.'

Cassidy, reviewing the book in *Nature*, described it as a good story, but insisted that 'as history it is incredible'. Rose dismisses it as 'entirely bogus' and 'a scholarly disaster'. Powers acknowledged ruefully, in a recent letter to the *Times Literary Supplement*, that he had failed to convince any historian who had pronounced upon the matter.

The play is not an attempt to adjudicate between these differing views of Heisenberg's personality, or these differing accounts of his activities. But it would have been impossible to write it without taking *some* view of Powers' version of events, so here, for what it is worth, is a brief summary of the case, and of my own hesitant view of it. The evidence is confused and contradictory, and making any sense of it involves balancing probabilities and possibilities almost as indeterminable as Heisenberg found events inside the atom.

*

Some of the evidence undoubtedly appears to support Powers's thesis in its stronger form, that Heisenberg deliberately sabotaged the project.

In the first place there are two scraps of direct testimony. One is a message brought to America in 1941 by a departing German Jewish academic called Fritz Reiche. It was from Fritz Houtermans, the German physicist who had just realised that if they could get a reactor going it would produce plutonium, and that plutonium would be a fissile alternative to the U-235 that they could not separate. Reiche testified later that he had passed it on to a group of scientists working at Princeton, including Wolfgang Pauli, John von Neumann, and Hans Bethe. As Rudolf Ladenburg, the physicist who arranged the meeting, recorded it afterwards, Houtermans wanted it to be known that 'a large number of German physicists are working intensively on the problem of the uranium bomb under the direction of Heisenberg', and that 'Heisenberg himself tries to delay the work as much as possible, fearing the catastrophic results of a success'.

Rose dismisses Houtermans as a proven liar, and records that Reiche later appeared to withdraw his belief in

Heisenberg's opposition to the project. But neither of these objections seems immediately relevant to the consistency of Reiche's and Ladenburg's testimony.

The second scrap of evidence is even more direct, but much more dubious. Heisenberg's American editor, Ruth Nanda Anshen, records receiving a letter from him in 1970 in which he claimed that, 'Dr Hahn, Dr von Laue and I falsified the mathematics in order to avoid the development of the atom bomb by German scientists.'

The letter itself has apparently vanished from the record. Rose nonetheless accepts it as beyond doubt genuine, and sees it as a yet more blatant attempt at self-justification. It is not, however, called into evidence by Powers, even though it would appear to support his case, and he mentions it only in his notes, and with the greatest reserve. Jeremy Bernstein, who seems to me the best-informed and most fair-minded of all Heisenberg's critics, and whose book *Hitler's Uranium Club* will be relied upon in understanding the scientific considerations that follow, dismisses it as 'incredible' and 'a chimera'. It is entirely at odds with Heisenberg's careful moderation in all his other references to the matter, and the inclusion of Hahn and von Laue in the plot is nonsensical. Hahn was a chemist, not a physicist, and, as will be plain from what comes later, had no knowledge whatsoever of the relevant mathematics, while von Laue is famous as an outspoken opponent of Nazism who never worked on the German nuclear programme at all.

So much for the direct evidence, true or false. All the rest of the evidence is indirect, and relates to whether Heisenberg did actually have some understanding of the relevant physics and concealed it, or whether he failed out of ignorance. It centres on the question of critical mass, the amount of fissile material (U-235 or plutonium) large enough to support an explosive chain reaction. An estimate of this amount was crucial to the decision about proceeding with a serious nuclear weapons programme because of the enormous difficulty and expense of separating the U-235 from the U-238 that makes up the vast bulk of natural uranium, and the length of time it would take to develop a reactor capable of transmuting the uranium into plutonium. At the beginning of the war it was believed by scientists on both sides that the answer would be in tons, which put the possibility of producing it beyond practical consideration. The idea became imaginable only when two scientists working in Britain, Rudolf Peierls and Otto Frisch, did the calculation and realised quite how fast the reaction would go with fast neutrons in pure U-235, and consequently how little fissile material you would need: not tons but kilograms. (The various ironies associated with this are explored in the play, and I will not repeat them here.)

Powers argues that the idea never became imaginable in Germany because Heisenberg 'cooked up a plausible method of estimating critical mass which gave an answer in tons'. He believes that Heisenberg 'well knew how to make a bomb with far less, but kept the knowledge to himself'.

There is a certain amount of evidence that the German team did at one point arrive at a much lower figure for the critical mass – indeed, for one in kilograms, that bore some relation to the estimate made by Frisch and Peierls, and to the actual mass of the Hiroshima bomb (56 kg). Manfred von Ardenne, who was running an alternative nuclear programme for the German Post Office, later claimed in his memoirs that in the late autumn of 1941 he was informed independently by both Heisenberg and Hahn that they had worked out the critical mass for a U-235 bomb and found it to be about 10 kilograms. This information was subsequently withdrawn by von Weizsäcker, who told him that he and Heisenberg had decided that a U-235 bomb was impossible (because the heat of the reaction would expand the uranium too fast for it to continue). But Heisenberg, so far as I know, never commented on this, and von Weizsäcker, according to Bernstein, 'essentially denied' that any such conversation ever took place.

As Bernstein says, it is difficult to know what to make of all this – it is 'one of several brick walls anyone who studies this subject runs into'. I think it's difficult to take von Ardenne's recollection entirely literally. Hahn, as I noted before, plainly had no understanding of the mathematics, nor of any of the other issues involved, and, as we shall see, had to have them explained to him by Heisenberg later. On the other hand (and this story has more other hands than a Hindu god), in von Weizsäcker's report on the possibility of an American bomb programme, written in September 1941, he talked about the destructive effects of a bomb weighing 5 kg. Then again, in February 1942 a brief progress report for German Army Ordnance, authors unnamed, suggested without further explanation a critical mass of between 10 and 100 kg. And at the crucial meeting with Speer at Harnack House in June 1942, when Field Marshal Milch asked him how large an atomic bomb would have to be to destroy a city, Heisenberg replied, or so he said in his interview with Irving, that it, or at any rate its 'essentially active part', would have to be 'about the size of a pineapple'.

In the end, though, I believe that the crucial piece of evidence lies elsewhere, in a source that was denied to everyone who wrote about Heisenberg until recently – the transcripts of the Farm Hall recordings. Bernstein, Powers, and Rose were the first commentators to have access to them.

Though of course they still don't reach the same conclusions from them.

*

The story of Farm Hall is another complete play in itself. Sir Charles Frank, the British atomic physicist, in his admirably fair and clear introduction to the text of the transcripts that was published in Britain, regrets that they were not released in time for Dürrenmatt to make use of.

At the end of the war troops of the Alsos mission, to which Goudsmit was attached, made their way through what was left of the German front line and located the remains of the German reactor at Haigerloch, with the intention of finally reassuring themselves that Germany would not be able to spring some terrible nuclear surprise at the last moment. They also seized the team of scientists themselves,

making a special armed sortie to Urfeld, in Bavaria, to
collect Heisenberg from his home. Hechingen, the nearby
town where the team was based, and Haigerloch itself were
in the French sector. The scientists were abstracted secretly,
from under the noses of the French, and brought back to
Britain, where they were held, under wartime laws and
without anyone's knowledge, in a former Intelligence safe
house – Farm Hall, near Cambridge. The intention seems to
have been partly to prevent their passing on any atomic
secrets to either of our other two allies, the Russians and the
French; partly to forestall any discussion of the possibility of
nuclear weapons until we had completed and used our own;
and partly, perhaps, to save Heisenberg and the others from
the alternative solution to these problems proposed by one
American general, which was simply to shoot them out of
hand.

They were detained at Farm Hall for six months, during
which time they were treated not as prisoners but as guests.
Hidden microphones, however, had been installed, and
everything they said to each other was secretly recorded.
The existence of the transcripts from these recordings was
kept as secret as that of the prisoners. General Groves, the
head of the Allied bomb programme, quoted from them in
his memoirs (1962), and Goudsmit plainly had access to
them, which he drew upon in his book on Alsos, but the
British Government, perhaps to protect the feelings of the
former detainees, some of them now prominent in post-war
German science, perhaps merely out of its usual pathological
addiction to secrecy, continued to block the release of the
papers themselves. Even Margaret Gowing was refused
access when she wrote her official history of British atomic
policy in 1964, and David Irving was refused again, in spite
of strenuous efforts, for *The Virus House* in 1967. The ban was
maintained until 1992, when the Government finally gave
way to a combined appeal from leading scientists and
historians.

The German originals are lost, and the translation was
plainly done under pressure, with little feeling for colloquial
nuance, but the transcripts are direct evidence of what

Heisenberg and the others thought when they were talking, as they believed, amongst themselves. The ten detainees represented a wide range of different attitudes. They ranged from Walther Gerlach, the Nazi Government's administrator of nuclear research, and Kurt Diebner, who had been a member of the Nazi party, to Max von Laue, who had been openly hostile to the regime, who had never worked on the atomic programme, and whose inclusion in the party seems on the face of it mysterious. Their conversations over the six-month period reflect a similarly wide range of attitudes and feelings. The general tone is pretty much what one might expect from any group of academics deprived of their liberty without explanation and cooped up together. There is, as one might suppose, quite a lot of complaining, scheming, and mutual friction.

One thing, though, seems to me to emerge quite clearly: for all practical purposes German thinking had stopped at a reactor, and there had been no eagerness at all to look beyond this to the possibility of weapons. Their shocked comments in the moment of unguarded horror that followed the announcement of Hiroshima are particularly revealing. The internees had been given the news by their (almost) endlessly sympathetic and urbane gaoler-cum-host, Major Rittner, at dinner-time, but Heisenberg had not believed it until he had heard it with his own ears on the BBC nine o'clock news. 'They were completely stunned,' reported Rittner, 'when they realised that the news was genuine. They were left alone on the assumption that they would discuss the position . . .'

'I was absolutely convinced,' says Heisenberg, in the conversation that followed, 'of the possibility of our making an uranium engine [reactor] but I never thought that we would make a bomb and at the bottom of my heart I was really glad that it was to be an engine and not a bomb. I must admit that.' Weizsäcker says that he doesn't think that they should make excuses now for failing, 'but we must admit that we didn't want to succeed.' Gerlach: 'One cannot say in front of an Englishman that we didn't try hard enough. They were our enemies, although we sabotaged the war. There are some things that one knows and one can discuss together but that one cannot discuss in the presence of Englishmen.'

In a letter written fourteen years later von Laue complained that, during their conversations at table in the following weeks, 'the version was developed that the German atomic physicists really had not wanted the atomic bomb, either because it was impossible to achieve it during the expected duration of the war or because they simply did not want to have it at all.' Von Laue's account of the elaboration of this sanitised 'version' (*Lesart* in German) has been seized upon by unsympathetic commentators, and contrasted with the encouraging prospects for atomic weapons that some of the physicists had undoubtedly held out to the Nazi authorities at various times during the earlier part of the war.

Well, we all reorganise our recollections, consciously or unconsciously, as time goes by, to fit our changed perceptions of a situation, and no doubt Heisenberg and his fellow-detainees did the same. But Bernstein locates the origins of the *Lesart* in those immediate reactions to the announcement of Hiroshima on the nine o'clock news. If this is so then I can only say that the team began to get their story together with quite remarkable spontaneity, speed, presence of mind, and common purpose. If they all thought as fast as this, and co-operated as closely, it's even more surprising that they didn't get further with the bomb.

To me, I have to say, those immediate and unprepared reactions suggest quite strongly that the first part of Powers's thesis, at any rate, is right, and that there *had* been the 'fatal lack of zeal' that he diagnosed. Perhaps Gerlach's claim, unchallenged by the others, that they had actually 'sabotaged the war' suggests at the very least a consciousness that quite a lot of stones had been left unturned.

*

But do the transcripts support Powers's contention that Heisenberg 'cooked up a plausible method of estimating critical mass which gave an answer in tons, and that he well knew how to make a bomb with far less, but kept the knowledge to himself'?

One preliminary point needs to be cleared out of the way first: the question whether Heisenberg understood an even more fundamental point, the difference between a reactor (which is operated by slow neutrons in natural uranium, or some other mixture of U-238 and U-235) and a bomb (which functions with fast neutrons in pure U-235 or plutonium). Goudsmit, who plainly had access to the transcripts when he wrote his book on Alsos, seems to have thought they supported his view that Heisenberg didn't. Before the transcripts were published Rose shared Goudsmit's dismissive view.

But, according to the transcripts, what Heisenberg tells Hahn that same night, when Gerlach has retired to sob in his room, and they are finally alone together, is that 'I always knew it could be done with 235 with fast neutrons. That's why 235 only [presumably = "only 235"] can be used as an explosive. One can never make an explosive with slow neutrons, not even with the heavy water machine [the German reactor], as then the neutrons only go with thermal speed, with the result that the reaction is so slow that the thing explodes sooner, before the reaction is complete.'

Bernstein (unlike Goudsmit) reads this and what follows as showing that Heisenberg *did* understand the difference between a reactor and a bomb, 'but that he did not understand either one very well – certainly not the bomb'. Rose now seems to accept that Heisenberg's remarks do indicate that he realised the bomb would have to be fissioned with fast neutrons (though he shows that in the past Heisenberg had been toying with the idea of some kind of vast exploding reactor).[1]

---

[1] Bernstein takes the trouble to explain in his book what few other commentators do – the difference between slow and fast neutrons: 'By definition, slow neutrons move with speeds of the order of a few kilometers a second, about the speeds that molecules at room temperature move in a gas. That is why these neutrons are also referred to as thermal. Fast neutrons, the kind that are emitted in many nuclear processes, move at speeds of tens of thousands of kilometers a second.'

This same conversation between Heisenberg and Hahn, when they were alone together on that terrible night, seems to me also to resolve the question of Heisenberg's understanding of the critical mass beyond any reasonable doubt. He takes Hahn through what he believes to be the relevant calculation and tells him that the answer is 'about a ton'. I can't see any earthly reason why he should be rehearsing a fabricated calculation or a fabricated answer at this stage, in a private conversation with someone he seems to have trusted, after the German team are out of the race and in custody, and after someone else has in any case already built the bomb. If he had had the right calculation and the right answer up his sleeve all the time, now would surely have been the moment to produce them. I find it much more plausible that he was telling the simple truth when he said to Hahn just before this that 'quite honestly I have never worked it out as I never believed one could get pure 235'.

Earlier on in the evening, it's true, when everyone was present during the conversation immediately after the news bulletin, Hahn says to Heisenberg: 'But tell me why you used to tell me that one needed 50 kilograms of 235 in order to do anything.' (To which Heisenberg replies that he wouldn't like to commit himself for the moment.) This does seem to suggest that he *had* made a calculation of some sort earlier, as von Ardenne claimed – though it also surely destroys once and for all the improbable proposition that Hahn had been involved in it, or had made some kind of estimate of his own. Perhaps Heisenberg had made not so much a calculation as some kind of guess or estimate. Even if it *was* a serious calculation, it seems most unlikely that it was the right calculation, or that it was one he had adhered to.

This is made clear to me (at last) by Jeremy Bernstein. I should explain that when I first read the Farm Hall transcripts, before I wrote the play, I was using the bare uncommented text published in Britain, unaware that there was also a completely different edition published in the US, incorporating Bernstein's detailed commentary. After the

play was produced and published he was kind enough to
send me it, and it illuminated a great many matters that I
had not understood before. These are after all scientists
talking to scientists, and they are reported verbatim with all
the ellipses of spoken conversation, and with a further haze
cast over the proceedings by translation. Bernstein is both a
distinguished journalist and a professor of physics, and he
has a long acquaintance with the history of atomic research.
(He recalls being given the bare plutonium core of a bomb
to hold on the Nevada test site in 1957; 'it was slightly warm
to the touch, since plutonium is marginally radioactive.') He
has a thorough understanding of the scientific issues
involved, and is the ideal guide to the physics – though a
slightly less percipient one, I think, to the psychology of the
physicists.

I'm pleased to discover for a start that he takes the same
view of Heisenberg's admission to Hahn about never having
worked out the critical mass. He believes that it has to be
taken at its face value, and he asks how it can be reconciled
with the figure of 50 kg recalled by Hahn. He demonstrates
that when Heisenberg attempts to do the calculation for
Hahn he 'gets it wrong at every level' – he does the
arithmetic wrong, and is in any case doing the wrong
arithmetic. 'Knowing how scientists work,' says Bernstein, 'I
find it implausible that he ever did the calculation correctly
before. One can imagine even a Heisenberg forgetting a
number – he was, in any case, not very good with numbers
– but it is very difficult to imagine his forgetting a general
method of calculation, a method that once led him to a
more reasonable answer.'

The calculation of the critical mass is not the only thing
that Heisenberg got wrong that night. Even when he
revealed to Hahn that he understood how the critical mass
could be reduced by the use of a reflective shield he
suggested a material, carbon, that would have had the
opposite effect to the one intended. Carbon is a good
moderator for a reactor, and Heisenberg's proposing it for
the 'tamper' in a bomb, says Bernstein, 'shows he was
thinking like a reactor physicist, which, for the last two years,

he was'.

These were of course Heisenberg's first thoughts off the top of his head in the wake of Hiroshima. A week later, with the help of what few details the newspapers had given of the two bombs, Heisenberg offered all his fellow-internees a lecture in which he presented a complete and considered account of how the Allies had done it. The inclusion in the lecture of quite fundamental matters, argues Powers, together with the questions which his hearers asked, make it clear that it was all news to everyone present except his closest associates. 'What the Farm Hall transcripts show unmistakably,' he says, 'is that Heisenberg did not explain basic bomb physics to the man in charge of the German bomb program [Gerlach] until after the war was over.' They 'offer strong evidence that Heisenberg never explained fast fission to Gerlach'. At the end of the lecture, says Powers, 'the German scientists, given a second chance, would have been ready to start building a bomb'.

Bernstein sees the lecture very differently. He demonstrates that Heisenberg's exposition is still marred by quite fundamental misconceptions. Heisenberg now seems to have 'the first inkling' of how to calculate the critical mass (though he still does the arithmetic wrong), but is not much nearer to the practicalities of building a bomb than his audience. What the novelty of a lot of this material suggests to Bernstein is simply that communications between the different sections of the German project were very poor.

As a non-scientist I can't offer any opinion on the physics. To my eyes, I have to say, Heisenberg does seem to have come a remarkably long way in a week – if, that is, he was starting more or less from scratch. And he surely must have been. It's really not plausible that he hadn't recollected more by this time if he actually had done the work. The conclusion seems to me inescapable: he hadn't done the calculation. If he had kept the fatal knowledge of how small the critical mass would be from anyone, as Powers argues, then it was from himself.

*

In the end, it seems to me, your judgment of Heisenberg comes down to what you make of his failure to attempt that fundamental calculation. Does it suggest incompetence or arrogance, as his detractors have claimed? It's possible. Even great scientists – and Bernstein agrees that Heisenberg was one of them – make mistakes, and fail to see possibilities that lesser men pick up; Heisenberg accepted that he had made a mistake in the formulation of uncertainty itself. And I think we have to accept Bernstein's judgment that, although he was the first person to be able to grasp the counter-intuitive abstraction of quantum mechanics, he was not so good at the practicalities of commonsense estimates and working arithmetic.

Or does the failure suggest something rather different? An unconscious reluctance to challenge the comforting and convenient assumption that the thing was not a practical possibility? Comforting and convenient, that is, if what he was trying to do was *not* to build a bomb. Is it all part of a general pattern of reluctance, as the first and more plausible part of Powers's thesis suggests? If so, you might wonder whether this reluctance was a state definite enough to be susceptible of explanation. Heisenberg was trapped in a seamless circle which explains itself: he didn't try the calculation because he didn't think it was worth doing – he didn't think it was worth doing because he didn't try it. The oddity, the phenomenon that requires explaining, is not this non-occurrence but its opposite – the escape of Frisch and Peierls from that same circle. It seems almost like a random quantum event; in which case, of course, it is no more explainable than its not happening.

After the war, certainly, Heisenberg was not just passively reluctant about any military application of nuclear power, but very actively so. In the 1950s, when there was a proposal to arm Federal Germany with nuclear weapons, he joined forces with Weizsäcker and others to fight a vigorous campaign that entirely and permanently defeated it.

There is also one small piece of evidence about his attitude during the war that Powers rather curiously doesn't comment on: the question of the cyclotron.

At the crucial meeting between Heisenberg and Speer in 1942, which seems finally to have scuppered all possibility of a German bomb, Heisenberg is reported to have emphasised the need to build a cyclotron. A cyclotron could have been used, as the cyclotrons in America were, for isotope separation, the great sticking-point in the German programme. In the account of this meeting in his memoirs Speer says: 'Difficulties were compounded, Heisenberg explained, by the fact that Europe possessed only one cyclotron, and that of minimal capacity. Moreover, it was located in Paris and because of the need for secrecy could not be used to full advantage.' Powers mentions this, but does not go on to the obvious corollary: that if Speer's recollection is accurate, then Heisenberg was plainly lying, because he knew perfectly well that there was a second cyclotron to hand – at Bohr's institute in Copenhagen. This would suggest that his apparent anxiety to lay his hands on a machine that might actually separate some U-235 was not quite what it seemed. Or, at the very least, that he placed Germany's war aims below his desire to protect Bohr's institute.

Perhaps Speer is simply wrong. It seems uncharacteristic of Heisenberg to have risked such a blatant falsehood, and he makes no mention of it in his own accounts of the meeting. All the same, when he went back to Copenhagen in 1944, after Bohr had fled, to adjudicate a German proposal to strip the institute of all its equipment, presumably including the cyclotron, he seems to have contrived to leave it even then still in Danish hands.

*

One of the forms of indeterminacy touched upon in the play is the indeterminacy of human memory, or at any rate the indeterminability of the historical record. There are various examples which I left out, for fear of making the play even more tangled than it is. Some, such as the difficulties about the amazingly realistic figure for the critical mass that von

Ardenne recollected being given by Heisenberg and Hahn in
1941, I have already mentioned in this Postscript. There
were others. A minor one concerns whether there were two
ships sent to load the Jews of Copenhagen for deportation,
as some witnesses recall, or a single one (named as the
*Wartheland*). A more significant point of dispute is the
drawing which Heisenberg did or didn't make for Bohr
during their meeting in 1941.

According to Hans Bethe, who was one of the team at Los
Alamos, Heisenberg drew a rough sketch to show Bohr the
work that was being done in Germany. Bohr evidently took
it to Los Alamos with him when he went, because Bethe
(and others) recall it being passed around at a meeting there.
Bethe told Powers that Bohr believed it represented a bomb;
but the consensus of opinion at the meeting was that it was a
reactor. However, Aage Bohr, Niels's son, a physicist himself
(and another Nobel prizewinner), who was with his father in
Copenhagen during Heisenberg's visit, and with him again
in Los Alamos, was absolutely insistent that there was no
drawing.

If the story is true it might help to explain Goudsmit's
insistence, in the teeth of the evidence from Farm Hall, that
Heisenberg couldn't tell the difference between a reactor and
a bomb. It would certainly cast doubt on Heisenberg's
recollection that the entire discussion with Bohr in 1941 took
place during the walk, and that Bohr broke off the
conversation almost as soon as it was broached. It seems
improbable to me that Heisenberg would have risked putting
anything down on paper, and if even so he had then I can't
see why he didn't seize upon it after the war, to support his
claim that he had hinted to Bohr at the German research on
a bomb. I suppose it's possible that Bohr made the sketch
himself, to illustrate to his colleagues at Los Alamos what he
thought Heisenberg was getting at, but the truth of the
matter seems to be irretrievable.

*

I have had many helping hands with this play, both before it was produced in London and since. Sir John Maddox kindly read the text for me, and so did Professor Balázs L. Gyorffy, Professor of Physics at Bristol University, who made a number of corrections and suggestions. I am also indebted to Finn Aaserud, the Director of the Niels Bohr Archive in Copenhagen, and to his colleagues there, for much help and encouragement. Many scientists and other specialists have written to me after seeing the play on the stage. They have mostly been extraordinarily generous and supportive, but some of them have put me right on details of the science, for which I am particularly grateful. They also pointed out two mathematical errors so egregious that the lines in question didn't make sense from one end to the other – even to me, when I re-read them. All these points have now been addressed, though I'm sure that other mistakes will emerge. So much new material has come to hand, in one way or another, that I extensively overhauled and extended this Postscript to coincide with the production of the play in New York.

One matter of dispute that I have not been able to resolve completely concerns the part played by Max Born in the introduction of quantum mechanics. The matter was raised (with exemplary temperance) by his son, Gustav Born, who was concerned about the injustice he felt I had done to his father's memory. I was reluctant to make the play any more complex than it is, but I have since made adjustments both to the play itself and to this Postscript which go at any rate some way to meeting Professor Born's case. We are still at odds over one line, though, in which Heisenberg is said to have 'invented quantum mechanics'. I am quoting the judgment of other physicists here (including one not especially sympathetic to Heisenberg), but I realise that it is a huge over-simplification, and that it seems to compound the original injustice committed when Heisenberg was awarded the Nobel Prize in 1932 'for the creation of quantum mechanics', while Born had to wait another 22 years to have his part acknowledged in the same way. The trouble is that I have not yet been able to think of another way of putting it briefly enough to work in spoken dialogue.

The American physicist Spencer Weart, in a letter to Finn
Aaserud, very cogently pointed out that the calculation of the
critical mass was much harder than I've made it seem for
Heisenberg once Bohr has suggested it to him. 'Perrin failed
to get it and his publication of a ton-size critical mass subtly
misled everyone else, then Bohr and Wheeler failed,
Kurchatov failed, Chadwick failed, all the other Germans
and Russians and French and British and Americans missed
it, even the greatest of them all for such problems, Fermi,
tried but missed, everyone except Peierls . . . Physics is hard.'

Some correspondents have also objected to Heisenberg's
line about the physicists who built the Allied bomb, 'Did a
single one of them stop to think, even for one brief moment,
about what they were doing?', on the grounds that it is
unjust to Leo Szilard. It's true that in March 1945 Szilard
began a campaign to persuade the US Government not to
use the bomb. A committee was set up – the Committee on
Social and Political Implications – to allow the scientists
working on the project to voice their feelings, and Szilard
also circulated a petition among the scientists, 67 of whom
signed it, which mentioned 'moral considerations', though it
did not specify what exactly these were.

But the main stated reasons for Szilard's second thoughts
were not to do with the effects that the bomb would have on
the Japanese – he was worried about the ones it would have
on the Allies. He thought (presciently) that the actual use of
the bomb on Japan would precipitate an atomic arms race
between the United States and the Soviet Union. The
Committee's report (which Szilard himself seems to have
written) and the petition stressed the same points. By this
time, in any case, the bomb was almost ready. It had been
Szilard who urged the nuclear programme in the first place,
and at no point, so far as I know, while he worked for it (on
plutonium production) did he ever suggest any hesitation
about pursuing either the research or the actual manufacture
of the bomb.

I think the line stands, in spite of Szilard's afterthoughts.
The scientists had already presented their government with
the bomb, and it is the question of whether the German

scientists were ready or not to do likewise that is at issue in the play. If Heisenberg's team *had* built a bomb, I don't think they would have recovered very much moral credit by asking Hitler to be kind enough not to drop it on anyone – particularly if their objection had been the strain it might place upon post-war relations among the Axis powers.

*

One looming imponderable remains. *If* Heisenberg had made the calculation, and *if* the resulting reduction in the scale of the problem had somehow generated a real eagerness in both the Nazi authorities and the scientists, could the Germans have built a bomb? Frank believes that they could not have done it before the war in Europe was over – 'even the Americans, with substantial industrial and scientific advantage, and the important assistance from Britain and from ex-Germans in Britain did not achieve that (VE-Day, 8 May 1945, Trinity test, Alamogordo, 16 July 1945).' Speer (who as Armaments Minister would presumably have had to carry the programme out) suggests in his memoirs that it might have been possible to do it by 1945, if the Germans had shelved all their other weapons projects, then two paragraphs later more cautiously changes his estimate to 1947; but of course he needs to justify his failure to pursue the possibility. Powers makes the point that, whatever the timetable was, its start date could have been much earlier. Atomic energy in Germany, he argues, attracted the interest of the authorities from the first day of the war. 'The United States, beginning in June 1942, took just over three years to do the job, and the Soviet Union succeeded in four. If a serious effort to develop a bomb had commenced in mid-1940, one might have been tested in 1943, well before the Allied bomber offensive had destroyed German industry.'

If this 'serious effort' had begun only after Heisenberg's visit to Copenhagen, as the play suggests might have happened if the conversation with Bohr had gone differently, then even this timetable wouldn't have produced a bomb until late 1944 – and by that time it was of course much less

likely that German industry could have delivered. In any
case, formidable difficulties remained to be overcome. The
German team were hugely frustrated by their inability to
find a successful technique for isolating U-235 in any
appreciable quantity, even though the experimental method,
using Clusius-Dickel tubes, was of German origin. They
could have tried one of the processes used successfully by the
Allies, gaseous diffusion. This was another German
invention, developed in Berlin by Gustav Hertz, but Hertz
had lost his job because his uncle was Jewish. (It was,
incidentally, the delays in getting the various American
isotope-separation plants to function which meant that the
Allied bomb was not ready in time for use against Germany.)

The failure to separate U-235 also held up the reactor
programme, and therefore the prospect of producing
plutonium, because they could not separate enough of it
even for the purposes of enrichment (increasing the U-235
content of natural uranium), so that it was harder to get the
reactor to go critical. The construction of the reactor was
further delayed because Walther Bothe's team at Heidelberg
estimated the neutron absorption rates of graphite wrongly,
which obliged the designers to use heavy water as a
moderator instead. The only source of heavy water was a
plant in Norway, which was forced to close after a series of
attacks by Norwegian parachutists attached to Special
Operations Executive, American bombers, and the
Norwegian Resistance. Though perhaps, if a crash
programme had been instituted from the first day of the war,
enough heavy water might have been accumulated before
the attacks were mounted.

If, if, if. . . . The line of ifs is a long one. It remains just
possible, though. The effects of real enthusiasm and real
determination are incalculable. In the realm of the just
possible they are sometimes decisive.

*

Anyone interested enough in any of these questions to want
to sidestep the fiction and look at the historical record should
certainly begin with:

Thomas Powers: *Heisenberg's War* (Knopf, 1993; Cape, 1993)

David Cassidy: *Uncertainty: The Life and Science of Werner Heisenberg* (W H Freeman, 1992)

Abraham Pais: *Niels Bohr's Times* (OUP, 1991) – Pais is a fellow nuclear physicist, who knew Bohr personally, and this, in its highly eccentric way, is a classic of biography, even though Pais has not much more sense of narrative than I have of physics, and the book is organised more like a scientific report than the story of someone's life. But then Bohr notoriously had no sense of narrative, either. One of the tasks his assistants had was to take him to the cinema and to explain the plot to him afterwards

Werner Heisenberg: *Physics and Beyond* (Harper & Row, 1971) – in German, *Der Teil und das Ganze*. His memoirs

Jeremy Bernstein: *Hitler's Uranium Club, the Secret Recordings at Farm Hall,* introduced by David Cassidy (American Institute of Physics, Woodbury, New York, 1996)

or the British edition of the transcripts:

*Operation Epsilon, the Farm Hall Transcripts,* introduced by Sir Charles Frank (Institute of Physics Publishing, 1993)

Also relevant:

Heisenberg: *Physics and Philosophy* (Penguin, 1958)

Niels Bohr: *The Philosophical Writings of Niels Bohr* (Oxbow Press, Connecticut, 1987)

Elisabeth Heisenberg: *Inner Exile* (Birkhauser, 1984) – in German, *Das politische Leben eines Unpolitischen*. Defensive in tone, but revealing about the kind of anguish her husband tended to conceal from the world; and the source for Heisenberg's ride home in 1945

David Irving: *The German Atomic Bomb* (Simon & Schuster, 1968) – in UK as *The Virus House* (Collins, 1967). The story of the German bomb programme

Paul Lawrence Rose: *Heisenberg and the Nazi Atomic Bomb Project* (U of California Press, 1998)

*Records and Documents Relating to the Third Reich, II German Atomic Research, Microfilms DJ29-32.* (EP Microform Ltd, Wakefield) – Irving's research materials for the book, including long verbatim interviews with Heisenberg and others. The only consultable copy I could track down was in the library of the Ministry of Defence

*Archive for the History of Quantum Physics*, microfilm. Includes the complete correspondence of Heisenberg and Bohr. A copy is available for reference in the Science Museum Library. Bohr's side of the correspondence is almost entirely in Danish, Heisenberg's in German apart from one letter

Leni Yahil: *The Rescue of Danish Jewry* (Jewish Publication Society of America, Philadelphia, 1969)

There are also many interesting sidelights on life at the Bohr Institute in its golden years in:

French & Kennedy, eds: *Niels Bohr, A Centenary Volume* (Harvard, 1985)

and in the memoirs of Hendrik Casimir, George Gamow, Otto Frisch, Otto Hahn, Rudolf Peierls, and Victor Weisskopf.

For the subsequent challenges to the Copenhagen Interpretation:

David Deutsch: *The Fabric of Reality* (Allen Lane, 1997)

Murray Gell-Mann: *The Quark and the Jaguar* (W H Freeman, 1994; Little, Brown, 1994)

Roger Penrose: *The Emperor's New Mind* (OUP, 1989)

The actual 'two-slits' experiment was carried out by Dürr, Nonn, and Rempe at the University of Konstanz, and is reported in *Nature* (3 September 1998). There is an accessible introduction to the work in the same issue by Peter Knight, and another account of it by Mark Buchanan (boldly entitled 'An end to uncertainty') in *New Scientist* (6 March 1999).

# POST-POSTSCRIPT

I made a number of changes to the text of the play, as I have explained above, in response to suggestions and criticisms I received during the run of the play in London, and to new material I came across. The production in New York, however, opened up a much broader and more fundamental debate. A number of commentators expressed misgivings about the whole enterprise. Paul Lawrence Rose, the most outspoken of the play's critics, even managed to detect in it a 'subtle revisionism . . . more destructive than Irving's self-evidently ridiculous assertions – more destructive of the integrity of art, of science, and of history'.

One of the most frequent complaints about the play in America was that I should have laid more stress on the evils of the Nazi regime, and in particular upon the Holocaust; it was pointed out that Heisenberg's visit to Copenhagen in 1941 coincided with the Wannsee Conference. It was argued that I should have put the visit in the context of a number of subsequent trips he made during the course of the war to other occupied countries. It was also felt that I should have laid more stress than I did on Heisenberg's stated view that Germany's conquests, at any rate in Eastern Europe, were justified, and that her victory over Russia was to be welcomed.

With hindsight, I think I accept some of these criticisms. I should perhaps have had Heisenberg justify Germany's war aims on the Eastern front direct, instead of having Bohr refer to his arguments in one angry but passing aside. I should perhaps have found some way to make the parallel with all the other trips that were found offensive, and about whose purpose there was none of the mystery which had seemed to attach to the one to Copenhagen.

About a greater stress on the evil of the Nazi regime I'm not so sure. I thought that this was too well understood to need pointing out. It is after all the *given* of the play; this was precisely why there was (or should have been) a problem facing Heisenberg, and us in understanding him. In any case, the play returns to the persecution of Jews in

Nazi Germany again and again, from the suppression of so-called 'Jewish physics' (relativity) to the enforced flight of all the Jewish physicists, the death of Goudsmit's parents in Auschwitz, and the attempt by the SS to deport the Jewish population of Denmark to the death camps, which Margrethe Bohr describes as 'that great darkness inside the human soul . . . flooding out to engulf us all'.

Some of the criticisms were even more radical. The play turns on the difficulty of determining why Heisenberg made his trip. For a number of commentators there was no problem at all – they knew the correct explanation for certain; though what that explanation was varied from one to another. For some it was Heisenberg's desire to persuade Bohr of the rightness of Germany's war aims and of its inevitable victory; for Rose and others, he was on a spying mission, to find out through Bohr if the Allies were also working on an atomic bomb.

I agree that Heisenberg may have wished to present the German case to Bohr; but he surely didn't go all the way to Copenhagen *just* to do that. I also agree about the spying. But then so does my Heisenberg. He tells Bohr that he wanted 'some hint, some clue' about whether there was an Allied nuclear programme. This seems to me to be common sense; he would have had to be insanely incurious not to seize any chance he could to find out whether the Allies might drop atomic bombs on his country. There is surely no contradiction at all with what he himself claimed his purpose was – to discuss whether the German team were justified in working on a German weapon. Any information he could get about the other side's intentions would have been a prerequisite for deciding what to do.

Some criticisms I reject, and I should like to put the record straight. Professor Rose suggested that I had 'fantasized' Heisenberg's fear that he was in danger of his life from the Gestapo for talking to Bohr. Not so – I was simply expanding upon what the real Heisenberg said. Jonothan Logan, a physicist writing in *American Scientist*, dismissed as misleading the fictitious Bohr's assertion that in June 1942 Heisenberg had been slightly ahead of Fermi in

Chicago. The context makes plain that this was in terms of neutron multiplication, and the claim was based on what David Cassidy says in his biography of Heisenberg. The correctness of Cassidy's assessment was verified for me, after much inquiry on my part, by Al Wattenberg, one of the editors of Fermi's *Collected Papers*.

All these are at any rate debatable points. Other criticisms I found extremely difficult to make sense of – some even to credit. Professor Rose, who detected the subtle revisionism of the play, found a particularly sinister significance in one detail – the fictitious Heisenberg's remarking upon the neatness of the historical irony whereby the crucial calculation (of the critical mass), which persuaded the Allies of the possibility of building a nuclear weapon, was made by a German and an Austrian, driven into exile in Britain because they were Jewish. Professor Rose saw this as an attempt to blame 'the Jews' for the bomb's invention.

A little more extraordinary still was the view of the play taken by Gerald Holton, Professor of Physics and Professor of the History of Science Emeritus at Harvard. He saw it as being 'structured in good part' to reflect the thesis advanced by Powers, that Heisenberg had correctly calculated the critical mass, but concealed it by 'cooking up' a false result. By the time the play was produced in New York, he believed, I had been forced (by Bernstein) to lay this idea aside, so that I now had an 'unsolvable problem' with the motivation of the play.

I can only suppose that Professor Holton was misled because in the Postscript I speak warmly and gratefully about Powers's book. It has been much attacked, but I continue to admire the generosity of its tone, and the range of Powers's research. I also agree with the first part of his thesis (lack of zeal). But then so does Holton himself, and so, he says, does everyone else who has studied the matter. In the Postscript, however, I make abundantly clear that I don't accept Powers's view about the 'cooking up' and never did.

But you don't even need to read the Postscript to

discover this, because it's all over the play itself. The central argument turns on Heisenberg's confession to Otto Hahn that he had *not* attempted the calculation. By my count, there are something like thirty-five speeches devoted to establishing this, to asking why he hadn't attempted it, and to suggesting what might have happened if he had. How anyone could give the play even the most cursory glance and fail to notice this is difficult to understand.

Even harder to credit was the reaction in some quarters to the 'strange new quantum ethics' proposed by the fictitious Heisenberg. I suppose I should have erected a flashing 'IRONY' sign in front of it. The allusion is to his insight, in his original introduction of quantum mechanics, that physics should be limited to the measurement of what we could actually observe – the external effects of events inside the atom. We should need a similar kind of ethics, he suggests in my play, if we judged people purely on the external effects of their actions, without regard to their intentions. According to Professor Holton, Heisenberg 'exults' that under the new dispensation there would be a place in heaven even for him. Professor Holton fails to mention that Heisenberg also 'exults' that, under the new quantum ethical rules, there would also be a place in heaven for the SS man who seemed ready to murder him in 1945, simply because in the end he settled for a pack of American cigarettes instead. Jonothan Logan manages to believe that I am seriously proposing even the SS man's assumption into heaven.

Let me make it absolutely unambiguous: my Heisenberg is saying that we *do* have to make assessments of intention in judging people's actions. (The epistemology of intention is what the play is about!) He is saying that Bohr will continue to inspire respect and love, in spite of his involvement in the building of the Hiroshima and Nagasaki bombs; and that he himself will continue to be regarded with distrust in spite of his failure to kill anyone. The reaction of Holton, Rose, and others to the play is perhaps an oblique testimony to the truth of this judgement.

\*

One of the most striking comments on the play was made by Jochen Heisenberg, Werner Heisenberg's son, when I met him, to my considerable alarm, after the première of the play in New York. 'Of course, your Heisenberg is nothing like my father,' he told me. 'I never saw my father express emotion about anything except music. But I understand that the characters in a play have to be rather more forthcoming than that.'

This seems to me a chastening reminder of the difficulties of representing a real person in fiction, but a profoundly sensible indication of the purpose in attempting it, which is surely to make explicit the ideas and feelings that never quite get expressed in the confusing onrush of life, and to bring out the underlying structure of events. I take it that the nineteenth-century German playwright Friedrich Hebbel was making a similar point when he uttered his great dictum (one that every playwright ought to have in pokerwork over his desk): 'In a good play everyone is right.' I assume he means by this not that the audience is invited to approve of everyone's actions, but that everyone should be allowed the freedom and eloquence to make the most convincing case that he can for himself. Whether or not this is a universal rule of playwriting, it must surely apply to this particular play, where a central argument is about our inability, in our observation of both the physical world and the mental, ever to escape from particular viewpoints.

I suppose that this is what sticks in some people's throats – that my Heisenberg is allowed to make a case for himself – even to criticise others. His claims about his intentions are strongly contested by another character in the play, Margrethe Bohr. Neither Heisenberg nor Margrethe Bohr, so far as I can see, is presented as winning the argument. I don't see why my Margrethe shouldn't be allowed to express her suspicions of Heisenberg much more sharply and woundingly than the real Margrethe's habitual courtesy would ever have permitted, and I don't see why my Heisenberg shouldn't be free to express the deeper feelings

that the real Heisenberg remained silent about. Why
shouldn't he have the same conflicting loyalties and the
same mixed motives and emotions that we all have? Why
shouldn't he try to juggle principle and expediency, as we
all do? Why shouldn't he fear his country's defeat, and its
destruction by nuclear weapons? Why shouldn't he lament
its ruin and the slaughter of its citizens?

I can imagine it being asked how far I think this
principle should be carried. Do I believe that a fictitious
Hitler should be accorded the same privileges? I can see all
the problems of exhibiting Hitler on the stage, but I can't
see any point in attempting it at all if he is to be simply an
effigy for ritual humiliation. Why should we be asked to
endure a representation of his presence if he doesn't offer
us some understanding of what was going on inside his
head from his own point of view? The audience can surely
be trusted to draw its own moral conclusions.

*

The most surprising result of the debate set off by the
production of the play, though, has been the release of the
Bohr documents.

I was told privately about the existence of at any rate
one of the documents at a symposium on the play
organised in Copenhagen by the Niels Bohr Archive in the
autumn of 1999. Heisenberg had made public his own
version of the 1941 meeting with Bohr, chiefly in two
places: a memorandum written in 1957 to Robert Jungk,
who was preparing the material for *Brighter Than a Thousand
Suns*, and his memoirs, published in 1969. Bohr, however,
had never publicly given his side of the story, and
historians had been obliged to rely upon what other people
(chiefly his son Aage – also a physicist, and later a Nobel
prizewinner himself – and his colleague Stefan Rozental)
recalled him as saying about it.

In 1957, however, Bohr had apparently been so angered
by Heisenberg's version, when he read it in Jungk's book,
that he had written to Heisenberg, dissenting and giving his

own account. He had never sent the letter, though, and at his death in 1962 it had been placed in the Archive by his family, not to be released for another fifty years. This was all my informant was prepared to tell me.

I said nothing about this because I believed that I had been told in confidence. The existence of the letter was first publicly mentioned, so far as I know, by Professor Holton, at a further symposium on the play organised in New York in March 2000 on the occasion of its production there. He said that he had actually seen the letter – he had been shown it by the Bohr family. He felt bound not to divulge its contents, but I recall him as promising that when it was finally made public, in 2012, it would entirely change our view of the meeting.

Now the cat was out of the bag, and at yet another symposium on the play, at the Niels Bohr Archive in September 2001, it was announced that the Bohr family had decided to release the letter early. It also turned out that there was not just the one letter but various alternative drafts and notes relating to it. When they were finally published on the web in February 2002, the whole question of the visit was accorded even wider attention in the press than ever before.

The documents seem to me to bear out remarkably well the very detailed reconstruction made of Bohr's attitude by Powers from other sources. The most surprising thing to me in Bohr's first attempt at the letter is its remarkably sharp tone – particularly coming from a man so celebrated for his conciliatoriness:

> I think that I owe it to you to tell you that I am greatly amazed to see how much your memory has deceived you . . .
>
> Personally, I remember every word of our conversations, which took place on a background of extreme sorrow and tension for us here in Denmark. In particular, it made a strong impression both on Margrethe and me, and on everyone at the Institute that the two of you spoke to, that you and Weizsäcker expressed your definite conviction that Germany would

win and that it was therefore quite foolish for us to
maintain the hope of a different outcome of the war and
to be reticent as regards all German offers of
cooperation. I also remember quite clearly our
conversation in my room at the Institute, where in vague
terms you spoke in a manner that could only give me
the firm impression that, under your leadership,
everything was being done in Germany to develop
atomic weapons and that you said that there was no
need to talk about details since you were completely
familiar with them and had spent the past two years
working more or less exclusively on such preparations. I
listened to this without speaking since [a] great matter
for mankind was at issue in which, despite our personal
friendship, we had to be regarded as representatives of
two sides engaged in mortal combat.

It is a revelation to have all this in Bohr's own voice, and I
wish it had been available when I wrote the play. I
recognise that the real Bohr remained much angrier for
much longer than my character, that he claimed to have
paid much closer attention to what Heisenberg said, and
that he claimed to recall it much more clearly.

Does it really modify our view of what Heisenberg said,
though, and of what his intentions were?

Slightly, I think, but not fundamentally. There has never
been any disagreement, for a start, that Heisenberg publicly
told various people at the Institute that Germany was going
to win the war, and that her aims, at any rate in the East,
were justified. Then again, Aage and Rozental were both
already on record as recalling Bohr's saying that Heisenberg
had talked about the military applications of atomic energy.
According to Aage, 'My father was very reticent and
expressed his scepticism because of the great technical
difficulties that had to be overcome, but he had the
impression that Heisenberg thought that the new
possibilities could decide the outcome of the war if the war
dragged on.' According to Rozental: 'I can only remember
how excited Bohr was after that conversation and that he
quoted Heisenberg for having said something like, "You

must understand that if I am taking part in the project then it is in the firm belief that it can be done."'

The letter, however, is the first direct confirmation that Bohr believed he was being urged to accept German 'offers of cooperation', which is what Weizsäcker suspected he may have understood Heisenberg to be suggesting. It's not clear from the letter what Bohr thought this 'co-operation' would entail, and the recollection may not be entirely at odds with what Weizsäcker recalls Heisenberg as telling Bohr – that he ought to establish contact with the staff of the German Embassy for his own safety.

Some of the differences between Bohr's account of the meeting and Heisenberg's are less clear-cut than Bohr's indignation makes them appear. According to Heisenberg, in his memorandum to Jungk, he told Bohr he knew that the use of uranium fission for making weapons was 'in principle possible, but it would require a terrific technical effort, which one can only hope cannot be realized in this war'. Bohr, he said, was shocked, 'obviously assuming that I had intended to convey to him that Germany had made great progress in the direction of manufacturing atomic weapons'. This is not all that different in substance, it seems to me, from what Bohr recalls.

The same is true when Bohr goes on to dispute Heisenberg's interpretation of his reaction:

> That my silence and gravity, as you write in the letter, could be taken as an expression of shock at your reports that it was possible to make an atomic bomb is a quite peculiar misunderstanding, which must be due to the great tension in your own mind. From the day three years earlier when I realized that slow neutrons could only cause fission in Uranium 235 and not 238, it was of course obvious to me that a bomb with certain effect could be produced by separating the uraniums . . . If anything in my behaviour could be interpreted as shock, it did not derive from such reports but rather from the news, as I had to understand it, that Germany was participating vigorously in a race to be the first with atomic weapons.

The difference between the 'shock' that Heisenberg diagnosed and the more dignified 'silence and gravity' that Bohr himself recalled dissolves a little in a later draft of the letter, where Bohr refers to his reaction as 'alarm'. His assertion that he already understood about the possibility of producing a weapon based on fission is moreover a simplification which is not quite supported by his subsequent behaviour. He had in fact up to that moment believed that it was a practical impossibility, because of the difficulty of separating the fissile U-235, and Heisenberg could not tell him why the balance of probability had now changed – because of the German team's realisation that a reactor, if they could get one going, would produce plutonium as an alternative. After Heisenberg's visit, according to Rozental, he was sufficiently shaken by Heisenberg's confidence to go back to the blackboard and rework all his calculations. Even so, he seems to have remained unconvinced when he got his guarded report on the meeting through to Chadwick, his contact with British intelligence, and said: 'Above all I have to the best of my judgment convinced myself that in spite of all future prospects any immediate use of the latest marvelous discoveries of atomic physics is impracticable.'

The real kernel of the apparent disagreement about the meeting emerges only in later drafts of the letter, where Bohr says that 'there was no hint on your part that efforts were being made by German physicists to prevent such an application of atomic science'. This appears to be a rebuttal of some claim made by Heisenberg. The belief that Heisenberg made some such claim seems to be widespread. Professor Holton suggests that my play is 'based in large part on Heisenberg's published claim that for him an impeding moral compunction may have existed about working on atomic energy'.

But nowhere, so far as I know, did Heisenberg ever make the claim that Bohr seems to have attributed to him. There is no mention of it in the memorandum to Jungk. Even in the expanded account of the meeting that he gave in his memoirs he remained extremely cautious:

I hinted that ... physicists ought perhaps to ask themselves whether they should work in this field at all ... An enormous technical effort was needed. Now this, to me, was so important precisely because it gave physicists the possibility of deciding whether or not the construction of atom bombs should be attempted. They could either advise their governments that atom bombs would come too late for use in the present war, and that work on them therefore detracted from the war effort, or else contend that, with the utmost exertions, it might just be possible to bring them into the conflict. Both views could be put forward with equal conviction ...

One might think this sounds a quite implausibly judicious rendering of anything he might have said. The fact remains, however, that he is not claiming to have made any efforts to prevent work on weapons. He is not even claiming that up to this point the German team had exercised the option of offering discouraging advice, only that they might at some point if they so chose. In any case, Heisenberg says that Bohr 'was so horrified by the very possibility of producing atomic weapons that he did not follow the rest of my remarks'.

Some reports on the release of the documents have suggested that they refute a claim made by Heisenberg to have offered Bohr a 'deal', whereby the German physicists would discourage their government from proceeding with nuclear weapons if Allied physicists would do likewise. I suppose the implication of Heisenberg's indeterminate phrase 'the physicists' is that this applied to the physicists on both sides, but the only evidence I can find for Heisenberg having made any more definite suggestion than this is in a part of the memorandum to Jungk which is quoted by Powers: 'I then asked Bohr once again if, because of the obvious moral concerns, it would be possible for all physicists to agree among themselves that one should not even attempt work on atomic bombs...' This might perhaps be interpreted as a tentative hint at some possible arrangement, though in the interview he gave to David Irving for *The Virus House* in 1965 he seems to be retreating even from this, and says merely that Bohr 'perhaps sensed that I should prefer it if physicists in the whole world would say: We will not make atom bombs'. The remark to Jungk was not quoted by him in his book, and so presumably not seen by Bohr in 1957. In his letter, in any case, Bohr makes no reference to any such claim, or to having understood any such offer at the time.

There are discrepancies in every other aspect of the evidence relating to this meeting, and it is scarcely surprising that there are some to be found between the two participants' own accounts. In both cases they are attempting to recollect something that happened sixteen years earlier, and their perceptions are inevitably coloured by strong feelings and conflicting loyalties. On the whole, I think, what's surprising is how slight the differences of substance are, and how readily most of them can be understood in the circumstances.

The most remarkable point of agreement, it seems to me now that I have had time to reflect upon it, was missed by everyone who wrote about the letters at the time of their release, myself included: Bohr's confirmation of Heisenberg's claim to have overridden all normal obligations of secrecy. Heisenberg did indicate to him, he agrees, that there was a German atomic programme; that he himself was involved in it; and that he now believed it in principle possible to build atomic weapons.

Whatever Heisenberg was officially licensed or ordered to do in Copenhagen, I cannot believe that it included revealing the existence of one of the most secret research programmes in Germany – least of all to an enemy alien who was known to be in contact with Allied scientists (Bohr was at this point still contributing to the US journal *The Physical Review*), and also to be under observation because of his hostile attitude to Nazism and his extensive help for its victims. Heisenberg must have done this of his own initiative, and he must have been aware that Bohr would pass the information on, if he possibly could, to his contacts in Britain or the US. This, it seems to me, goes a considerable way to supporting the account that Heisenberg subsequently gave of his intentions.

*

The only really clear-cut disagreement between the two accounts is about a circumstantial detail – where the meeting took place. Bohr talks about 'our conversation in my room at the Institute'. Heisenberg, on the other hand, recalls in his memoirs visiting the Bohrs' home in Carlsberg, and finally broaching 'the dangerous subject' on their evening walk. This version is reinforced by what he recalls of his attempt to reconstruct with Bohr the 1941 meeting when he returned to Copenhagen in 1947. He was convinced, he said, that the conversation had taken place during 'a nocturnal walk on Pile Allé', which is very close to Carlsberg, and four kilometres from the Institute. (Bohr at the time, according to Heisenberg, thought it had been in his study – but in his study at home in Carlsberg.)

Bohr himself lends some colour to the Carlsberg version by his remark in the letter that 'every word of our conversation . . . made a strong impression both on Margrethe and me'. It seems highly unlikely that Margrethe would have been present at any of the various meetings in the Institute; I don't think that any of the other participants mention her. Jochen Heisenberg recalls his father showing him the street where he said he had walked with Niels Bohr in 1941, though he can't now remember the name of it, only that it was tree-lined (which Pile Allé is).

There is a secondhand account of the meeting given to Thomas Powers by Ruth Nanda Anshen, Heisenberg's American editor, who said that she was told it by Bohr, and that his assistant Aage Petersen confirmed it. According to Powers, in *Heisenberg's War*, Bohr told Anshen that 'the invitation had cost him much agony – he wanted to sit down to dinner with Heisenberg, but his wife, Margrethe, objected, and Bohr couldn't make up his mind what to do. Finally his assistant Aage Petersen suggested that Bohr should write down his objections to Heisenberg's visit, then read them carefully a day or two later, and decide. This Bohr did; the old friendship seemed to him stronger than the objections, and he told his New York friend that he finally obtained Margrethe's agreement with a solemn promise to discuss only physics with Heisenberg – not politics.'

On the other hand Abraham Pais, Bohr's biographer, after making inquiries among Bohr's surviving colleagues just before his own death in 2000, concluded that Heisenberg had never been to the Bohrs' home.

Even Heisenberg's own testimony is not entirely consistent. According to his biographer, David Cassidy, he made an earlier statement in which he 'remembered that his most important talk with Bohr occurred one evening as they strolled along a tree-lined path in the large and secluded Faelledpark, just behind Bohr's institute'. Weizsäcker, who recalled that he met Heisenberg only ten minutes after the meeting with Bohr was over (the two men had parted company, he said, 'in a friendly way', but Heisenberg had immediately told him: 'I'm afraid it's gone completely wrong') agreed that it had taken place in the open air, but introduced another location altogether – Langelinie, the raised walk beside the harbour, miles from either Carlsberg or the Institute.

*

Some further light on this question was cast, nine months after the release of the Bohr documents, by the emergence of yet another letter. This one was written by Heisenberg, and revealed by Dr Helmut Rechenberg, the director of the Werner Heisenberg Archive in Göttingen.[1] The Heisenberg family, who released it, seem not to have taken in its implications earlier.

It makes no direct reference to the disputed conversation itself, but is a much more reliable guide to the

[1] In a Heisenberg Centenary Festschrift issued by the Sächsische Akademie der Wissenschaften. The letter was published in 2003 in a collection of his correspondence edited by his daughter Maria Hirsch.

circumstances surrounding it than the accounts we have
had so far, because it was written not sixteen years after
the event but during the week that Heisenberg was actually
there. In fact it's in three sections, dated respectively to
three different evenings – Tuesday (September 16, the day
after he arrived), Thursday, and Saturday – and it was
posted to his family in Leipzig as soon as he got back to
Berlin.

The letter clears up one small point of dispute completely.
Heisenberg *did* go to the house – and more than once. He
also records various visits to the Institute, and the sheer
number and variety of meetings that the two men had
during the week supports the claim that Heisenberg's chief
reason for making the trip was to see Bohr. The conflation
of the different occasions in the participants' memories also
probably explains some of the later discrepancies.

The first visit to the Bohrs was late on the Monday
evening, as soon as Heisenberg had got off the train from
Berlin. The sky, he recorded, was clear and starry, but in
the Bohrs' house he found rather darker weather. 'The
conversation swiftly turned to the human questions and
misfortunes of our time; about the human ones there was
spontaneous agreement; on the political questions I found it
difficult to cope with the fact that even in a man like Bohr,
thoughts, feelings, and hatred cannot be completely
separated.'

It is just possible that the fateful conversation occurred at
this first meeting, either in the house – where, said
Heisenberg, 'later I sat for a long time alone with Bohr' –
or later still, after midnight, when Bohr saw him to the
tram. But they were accompanied to the tram-stop by
Hans, one of Bohr's sons, who would surely have
remembered and remarked upon it if it had happened then.
And if Weizsäcker's recollection is even remotely accurate
then the conversation can't have occurred at any point
during this first meeting, because he himself arrived in
Copenhagen only on the Wednesday.

The most likely occasion was two days later, during
Heisenberg's second visit, on the Wednesday evening. (This

time there was a young Englishwoman present, who
'decently withdrew' during 'the unavoidable political
conversations, in which the role of defending our system of
course automatically fell upon me'.) Dr Rechenberg suggests
plausibly that Bohr accompanied Heisenberg alone part of
the way back to his hotel, where Weizsäcker was waiting
for him.

The real surprise of the letters, though, is that
Heisenberg was invited back to the Bohrs' home for a *third*
time, on the Saturday evening, three days after this (and
the conversation can't have occurred during this visit,
because this time Weizsäcker was accompanying him). 'It
was in many ways particularly nice,' wrote Heisenberg later
that same night. 'The conversation turned for a great part
of the evening around purely human problems. Bohr read
something aloud, I played a Mozart sonata (A major).'

The immediate rupture of the two men's friendship is
almost the only aspect of the story which has up to now
seemed reasonably unambiguous (I certainly take it for
granted in the play). Now even this turns out to be as
clouded as everything else.

Rechenberg suggests that it may have been at this
farewell meeting that Heisenberg and Weizsäcker urged
Bohr to maintain contact with the German Embassy. If so
it could have been Bohr's anger at this that coloured his
recollection of the earlier conversation. It is in any case
clear that the quarrel took the form it did only later, in the
recollection of the participants, as they reflected upon it –
probably also as the circumstances of the war got worse, as
the deepest horrors of the Nazi period were uncovered, and
as the actual development of nuclear weapons called into
question the two men's participation.

History, in other words, is not what happens when it
happens, but what seems to people to have happened when
they look back upon it.

*

I can't help being moved, though, by the picture that the new documents give of Bohr drafting and redrafting the text of the letter over the last five years of his life – and still never sending it. He was famous for his endless redrafting of everything he wrote, and here he was trying not only to satisfy his characteristic concern for the precise nuance, but also to reconcile that with his equally characteristic consideration for Heisenberg's feelings. There is a sad parallel with the account which Professor Hans-Peter Dürr gave, at the Heisenberg Centenary symposium in Bamberg last year, of Heisenberg's rather similar efforts to understand what had happened.

Professor Dürr, who worked for many years with Heisenberg in Göttingen after the war, said that Heisenberg had contined to love Bohr to the end of his life, and he recalled his going over the fatal meeting again and again, trying to work out what had happened. Professor Dürr offered what seems to me the most plausible common-sense estimate of Heisenberg's intentions that has yet been advanced. He thought that Heisenberg had simply wanted to have a talk. Heisenberg and Bohr had been so close that they could finish each other's sentences, and he assumed that he would have only to hint at what was on his mind for Bohr to grasp the significance of it. What he had entirely failed to grasp was that the situation had changed, and that Bohr's anger about the German occupation would make the old easy communication entirely impossible.

Whatever was said at the meeting, and whatever Heisenberg's intentions were, there is something profoundly characteristic of the difficulties in human relationships, and profoundly painful, in that picture of the two ageing men, one in Copenhagen and one in Göttingen, puzzling for all those long years over the few brief moments that had clouded if not ended their friendship. It's what their shades do in my play, of course. At least in the play they get together to work it out.

---

Overleaf: a diagram outlining *Copenhagen*'s scientific and historical background.

**From the beginnings of modern atomic theory to Hiroshima: an outline sketch of the scientific and historical background to the play.**

### Electrons

1895 Thomson discovers the electron, the extremely light, negatively charged particles orbiting inside the atom which give it its chemical properties.

### Quantum Theory

1900 Planck discovers that heat energy is not continuously variable, as classical physics assumes. There is a smallest common coin in the currency, the quantum, and all transactions are in multiples of it.

### The Nucleus

1910 Rutherford shows that the electrons orbit around a tiny nucleus, in which almost the entire mass of the atom is concentrated.

### Photons

1905 Einstein realises that light, too, has to be understood not only as waves but as quantum particles, later known as photons.

### The Quantum Atom.

1913 Bohr realises that quantum theory applies to matter itself. The orbits of the electrons about the nucleus are limited to a number of separate whole number possibilities, so that the atom can exist only in a number of distinct and definite states. (The incomplete so-called 'old quantum theory'.)

### Quantum mechanics

1925 Heisenberg abandons electron orbits as unobservable. Max Born finds instead a mathematical formulation in terms of matrices for what can be observed - the effects they produce upon the absorption and emission of light.

### Uncertainty

1927 Heisenberg demonstrates that all statements about the movement of a particle are governed by the uncertainty relationship: the more accurately you know its position, the less accurately you know its velocity, and vice versa.

### Matter as Waves

1924 De Broglie in Paris suggests that, just as radiation can be treated as particles, so the particles of matter can be treated as a wave formation.

### The Wave Equation

1926 Schrödinger finds the mathematical equation for the wave interpretation, and proves that wave and matrix mechanics are mathematically equivalent.

### The Copenhagen Interpretation

1928 Bohr relates Heisenberg's particle theory and Schrödinger's wave theory by the complementarity principle, according to which the behaviour of an electron can be understood completely only by descriptions in both wave and particle form. Uncertainty plus complementarity become established as the pillars of the Copenhagen (or 'orthodox') interpretation of quantum mechanics.

### Neutrons

1932 Chadwick discovers the neutron - a particle which can be used to explore the nucleus because it carries no electrical charge, and can penetrate it undeflected.

### Into the Nucleus

1932 Heisenberg opens the new era of nuclear physics by using neutron theory to apply quantum mechanics to the structure of the nucleus.

**Transmutation**

1934 Fermi in Rome bombards uranium with neutrons and produces a radio-active substance which he cannot identify.

**Identification**

1939 Hahn and Strassmann in Berlin identify the substance produced by Fermi's bombardment as barium, which has only about half the atomic weight of uranium.

**The Liquid Drop**

1937 Bohr explains the properties of the nucleus by analogy with a drop of liquid.

**Fission**

1939 Lise Meitner and Frisch in Sweden apply Bohr's liquid drop model to the uranium nucleus, and realise that it has turned into barium under bombardment by splitting into two, with the release of huge quantities of energy.

**The Neutrons Multiply**

1939 Bohr and Wheeler at Princeton realise that fission also produces free neutrons. These neutrons are moving too fast to fission other nuclei in U-238, the isotope which makes up 99% of natural uranium, and will fission only the nuclei of the U-235 isotope, which constitutes less than 1% of it.

**The Chain Reaction**

1939 Joliot in Paris and Fermi in New York demonstrate the release of two or more free neutrons with each fission, which proves the possibility of a chain reaction in pure U-235.

**The Critical Mass**

1940 Frisch and Peierls in Birmingham calculate, wrongly but encouragingly, the minimum amount of U-235 needed to sustain an effective chain reaction.

**The War**

1939 The Second World War begins, and Germany at once commences research into the military possibilities of fission.

**The Manhattan Project**

1942 The Allied atomic bomb programme begins.

**Germany Defeated**

1945 The Allied advance into Germany halts the atomic programme there.

**The Reactor**

1942 Fermi in Chicago achieves the first self-sustaining chain reaction, in a prototype reactor.

**The Bomb**

1945 The bomb is successfully tested in July, and in the following month used on Hiroshima.

# Notes

describe quantum behaviour – one was in terms of waves, the other was in terms of particles.

6 *Then the Nazis came to power*: Hitler became Chancellor of Germany on 30 January 1933.

*For years I had it down in my memory as October*: the fallibility of memory is a recurrent theme.

*A curious sort of diary memory is*: the characters move in and out of time-zones in a way that reflects this observation.

*September, 1941, Copenhagen*: the deft transitions in time depend on a non-naturalistic setting. 'This is not a naturalistic play,' the director Michael Blakemore has said. 'We're not trying to pretend that what we're seeing is real. The audience must listen to the arguments, empathise with the characters' emotions, and create the reality for themselves' (www.nucnews.net [9 April 2000]).

*Weizsäcker*: Carl Friedrich von Weizsäcker (1912– ). Theoretical physicist and influential younger colleague and friend of Heisenberg's. His father, Ernst, was the second highest official in Hitler's Foreign Office, who was sentenced to jail at Nuremberg. His brother Richard later became President of the Federal Republic of Germany (1984–94).

7 *Occupation of Poland*: Germany invaded Poland on 1 September 1939. Two days later Britain and France declared war on Germany.

*Christian Møller*: professor of mathematical physics in Copenhagen. Møller (1904–81) contributed to atomic and nuclear theory and wrote *The Theory of Relativity*.

8 *Our tanks are almost at Moscow*: Germany invaded Russia on 22 June 1941. On 19 September the Germans launched the Moscow offensive.

*the basement at Prinz-Albrecht-Strasse*: this was the headquarters of the SS in Berlin.

*White Jew*: in 1937, in the SS weekly *Das Schwarze Korps*, the Nobel prizewinner Johannes Stark attacked Heisenberg for being too indebted to 'Jewish' quantum physics. A 'white Jew' was a toxic term of abuse for a German who helped spread the Jewish 'spirit'.

9   *Still a professor*: Margrethe's testiness is essential in drawing out information for the audience.
   *Goudsmit*: Dutch-American physicist and scientific head of the Alsos mission, Samuel A. Goudsmit (1902–78) was responsible for arresting Heisenberg, and the other scientists detained at Farm Hall, at the end of the war.

10  *We'll stick to physics*: the subtle shifts in time and perspective are evident here, when Bohr talks about what he *thinks* will happen at the 1941 meeting.
   *So now here I am*: the encounter moves into the present tense. For the first few pages the Bohrs have shared the stage with Heisenberg without meeting him. Now the three of them are together.

11  *nuclear fission*: the splitting of a heavy atomic nucleus, which releases nuclear energy.
   *Wolfgang Pauli*: (1900–58), won the 1945 Nobel Prize for the 'exclusion principle' which explained the electronic make-up of atoms.
   *Otto Frisch*: (1904–79), nephew of Lise Meitner. The Nazi racial laws forced him to emigrate. He worked with Bohr in Copenhagen. With Meitner he wrote the paper that gave the first correct description of fission.
   *Lise Meitner*: during the thirties Meitner (1878–1968) and Otto Hahn investigated what happened to uranium when it was bombarded with neutrons. In 1939 Meitner and her nephew Otto Frisch realised that a new process – fission – had occurred.
   *Sommerfeld*: German physicist (1868–1951) Arnold Sommerfeld worked on quantum theory, making a significant contribution to Bohr's atomic theory by extending the theory to include elliptical paths for electrons.
   *Von Laue*: won the Nobel Prize for Physics in 1914 for his research on X-rays. Max von Laue (1879–1960) was bewildered by his detainment at Farm Hall after the Second World War. He had engaged in no war-related

research during the war.

*Wirtz*: German physicist, detained at Farm Hall. Karl Wirtz (1910–94) was an expert in heavy water and isotope separation.

*Harteck*: professor of physical chemistry. Paul Harteck (1902–85) was detained at Farm Hall. During the war he worked on heavy-water production and reactor construction.

12 *Otto Hahn*: a radiochemist, he worked with Lise Meitner for thirty years. Like the other detainees at Farm Hall, Hahn (1879–1968) learnt about the Hiroshima bomb during his internment. He also learnt that he had been awarded the Nobel Prize for Chemistry.

*Enrico Fermi*: made major contributions in experimental and theoretical physics. In 1934 Fermi (1901–54) showed that bombarding uranium with slow neutrons resulted in a radioactive substance (fission had taken place), but he did not realise quite what he had achieved. He later worked on the Manhattan Project at Los Alamos.

13 *And of course*: Margrethe steps out of the scene just as Heisenberg steps into it.

15 *A few months ago they started deporting*: two vast events lie, like shadows, behind the play – the Holocaust and the atomic bomb. In 1941 neither of these horrors had been realised.

16 *Silence again*: Margrethe comments on the scene in 1941 even as it is taking place, and then her memory flashes back to 1924.

17 *nuclei*: the nucleus is the central core of the atom, composed of protons and neutrons.

*deuterons*: the nucleus of a deuterium atom (deuterium is also known as heavy hydrogen).

*cyclotron*: invented in 1931 to smash atoms. It accelerates charged particles by means of a magnetic field. It is used to break down atoms or combine them. (See p. 124.)

*We mustn't jump to conclusions*: the next four lines, like a number of others, achieve a choric effect as if the three characters had joined together to become a single narrator.

18 *Schrödinger*: the Austrian physicist Erwin Schrödinger (1887–1961) formulated his wave equation in 1926 which used wave function as the mathematical expression for measuring the co-ordinates of a particle in space. (See also note to p.25.)

*I'm not teaching*: Heisenberg is not entirely candid about the work he is doing.

19 *Chadwick*: confirmed the existence of the neutron in 1932 and received the Nobel Prize for its discovery in 1935. During the war James Chadwick (1891–1974) headed the British atomic bomb project.

*Oppenheimer*: in 1942 J. Robert Oppenheimer (1904–67) was put in charge of the scientific side of the Manhattan Project.

*mesons*: a sub-particle of the atom.

25 *particle . . . goes through two different slits at the same time*: one of the mind-bending aspects of quantum mechanics is that when a particle is faced with the choice of going through one of two slits it appears to go through both of them. (Don't ask.) See also p.102.

*Schrödinger's wretched cat*: Bohr maintained that the position of a particle remains indeterminate until it has been observed. In response to this, Schrödinger posed a famous question that was of more interest to physicists than to cat lovers: if a cat were placed in a sealed box with some radioactive material, how could we know if or when the cat had died?

26 *Hendrik Casimir*: (1909–) made important contributions to applied mathematics, theoretical physics and low-temperature physics.

*George Gamow*: one of the originators of the big bang theory, a professor of physics, Gamow (1904–68) wrote popular science books.

29 *Christian and Harold*: see p.xlviii.

30 *Elsinore*: Hamlet's home. Heisenberg is a Hamlet figure, unable to decide what it is he should do. Elsinore becomes a term for the destructive impulses, the dark side of humanity, which recurs throughout the play.

32 *Goodbye:* the end of the first visit. What follows is the rival interpretations of that first meeting.
*John Wheeler*: American physicist (1911–). Working with Bohr in 1939 at Princeton, he realised that fission also produces free neutrons.

33 *neutron*: one of the two components of an atomic nucleus. Separated on its own, a neutron undergoes radioactive decay.
*isotope*: one of two or more atoms of the same chemical element, which have the same number of protons, but differ in the number of neutrons in the nucleus. From the Greek 'isos' (the same) and 'topos' (place).

37 *plutonium*: a man-made heavy metal, discovered at the University of California in 1940, formed by the radioactive decay of neptunium, that was ideal for use in nuclear weapons.

38 *Weisskopf*: leading theoretical physicist, Victor Weisskopf (1908–) was a Viennese Jew who emigrated to the US in 1937 and worked at Los Alamos from 1943.

40 *Geiger counters*: developed in 1928, the counters detect and measure radioactivity.

42 *It's just getting under way even as you and I are talking*: his mind moves forwards in time as well as backwards.

43 *Teller*: a Hungarian Jew, Edward Teller (1908–) went to the United States in 1935 and to Los Alamos in 1943 to work on a fusion weapon. He is known as the 'father of the H-bomb'. He has been caricatured in the movie *Dr Strangelove*.
*Szilard*: in 1934, four years before fission was identified, the Hungarian Leo Szilard (1898–1964) conceived the idea of a 'chain reaction', involving neutrons. In 1939 he warned Einstein of the possibility of a chain reaction. Einstein wrote to President Roosevelt (with Szilard's support) warning the President of the possibility

of an atomic arms race (see p.127).

48  *our meeting with Albert Speer*: Hitler's favourite architect, Speer, became Minister for Armaments and War Production. Heisenberg briefed him on nuclear research on 4 June 1942.

*the RAF have begun terror-bombing*: the RAF began its strategic bombing offensive on 15 May 1940. After the German bombing of London the RAF attacked Berlin on 25 August 1940.

50  *Hambro*: Sir Charles Hambro, a prominent banker and commander of SOE (Special Operations Executive). On 21 April 1945, after supper in a local hotel, Hambro and Perrin went into the cave at Haigerloch to inspect the nuclear pile that Heisenberg had been building.

*Perrin*: Michael Perrin, physicist and official of the British atomic programme. He discussed the German bomb programme with Bohr when Bohr reached England in 1943. He inspected Heisenberg's reactors at Haigerloch. He was one of those who received the weekly transcripts from Farm Hall.

53  *Another draft of the paper*: although the second attempt to explain the visit was heralded fifteen pages ago ('let's start all over again'), it starts here.

54  *And from those two heads*: in the final moment of the first act, Margrethe restates what is at stake.


*Act Two*

59  *Dirac*: Paul Dirac (1902–84), British physicist, best known for the Dirac Equation (1928). This gave a relativistic wave equation for electrons that replaced Schrödinger's non-relativistic equation in situations when relativity is a factor (for instance, high speed).

*de Broglie*: French physicist Louis de Broglie (1892–1987) was best known for his theory of wave-particle duality. In 1924 he hypothesised that particles should exhibit certain wave-like properties. He received the Nobel

Prize in 1929.

*Landau*: Lev Landau (1908–68), Russian physicist, who early on saw the possibility of a bomb.

*Uhlenbeck*: in the 1920s, George Uhlenbeck (1900–88), working with Goudsmit, introduced the idea of 'electron spin'.

*Stern*: an experimental physicist, Otto Stern (1888–1969) worked with Walther Gerlach, one of the Farm Hall detainees, on the influential 1922 atomic-beam experiment.

60 *Ehrenfest*: with Max Planck, Einstein and Bohr, Paul Ehrenfest (1880–1933) was a pioneer of the quantum revolution.

62 *Any more than*: Margrethe states a central theme in the play: how we can never understand one another's thoughts.

63 *Schrödinger's wave formulation*: see note to p.18.
*matrix mechanics*: the first formulation of quantum mechanics, made by Heisenberg in 1925, was presented in terms of mathematical matrices.

68 *photon*: in 1905 Einstein realised that light had to be understood not only as waves but as quantum particles, later known as photons.

70 *Klein*: Oskar Klein (1894–1977) joined Bohr in 1918 and later remarked on the great progress that Bohr had made in the early 1920s 'in spite of the abyss, whose depth he never ceased to emphasize, between the quantum theoretical mode of description and that of classical physics'.

75 *the plot against Hitler*: on 20 July 1944, at a conference at Hitler's headquarters at Rastenberg in East Prussia, Count von Stauffenberg left a suitcase bomb in a room where Hitler was holding a meeting. Hitler was not seriously injured. Many of the plotters and their relations were executed.

76 *Better to stay on the boat*: the question of what action people should take in desperate situations, and whether it is right to make a sacrifice that is heroic and

probably useless, parallels Heisenberg's dilemma in Nazi Germany.

82 *diffusion equation*: diffusion is the atomic process by which substances mix or spread. In a solid or liquid, diffusion can only take place when an atom or molecule acquires enough energy to jump to another place.

83 *Peierls*: working in Birmingham in the late-thirties, the German physicist Rudolf Peierls (1907–95) calculated that pure uranium 235 could make an atom bomb. A memo was sent to the British government. It was immediately classified as top secret and Peierls, an enemy alien, was not allowed to read the document he had written. Peierls later wrote about Heisenberg that 'though a brilliant theoretician he was always very casual about numbers'.

86 *One more draft*: in the play's three-act structure this is the beginning of the third act. From now on the play moves inside the characters' thoughts. Michael Blakemore said in an interview: 'The play moves away from science towards what Michael [Frayn] tells me is late-Wittgenstein – into a sort of philosophical position – where, having examined this meeting twice, in terms of history and in terms of science, the exhausted participants have to actually examine very specifically what happens when three people encounter one another' (www.nucnews.net [9 April 2000]).

89 *To leave him misunderstood*: this is as close as we get to the reason for the visit.

# Questions for Further Study

1. What is the dramatic purpose and function of the role of Margrethe in *Copenhagen*?
2. What are the advantages/disadvantages of staging the play as a discussion in an afterlife rather than as an imagined historical reconstruction?
3. 'I sometimes feel very envious of your cyclotron' (p.17). Do you need to be able to make sense of the science to make sense of *Copenhagen*?
4. 'The emotional currents between the three characters in *Copenhagen* give the play its questing energy.' Discuss.
5. The language of indeterminacy, alternative narratives, alternative histories belongs to the realm of literary theory as well as science. To what extent does *Copenhagen* suggest that the separation of the spheres of science and literature (the 'Two Cultures' idea) is a myth?
6. 'The play deals with politics on the largest scale imaginable, and personal relationships at their most private and unspoken.' How successfully does Frayn succeed in dramatising the relationship between the political and the personal in *Copenhagen*?
7. Some critics felt that *Copenhagen* would fare better as a play for radio. Give your reasons for agreeing or disagreeing with this view.
8. 'No one is going to develop a weapon based on nuclear fission' (p.11). How does Frayn deploy historical and scientific knowledge which is available to us but not to the protagonists?
9. To what extent does the play seem to be preoccupied with moral relativity or moral indeterminacy, given that Heisenberg describes Bohr towards the end of the play as a 'good' man?

10. In the commentary, Michael Frayn is quoted as saying that the play is 'about audiences' (p. xxxviii). What do you think he means and how might this affect the staging of *Copenhagen*?

11. 'I wanted to get into the question of how we know why we do what we do. We can't come to any moral judgements of people or ourselves until we can make some estimation of motivations. The difficulties of doing this point to a fundamental difficulty in making moral judgements' (Michael Frayn). How essential are the particular people and situations in the play to the philosophical problems posed and how successfully does *Copenhagen* deal with them?

12. What kind of moral or other issues does *Copenhagen* raise in portraying a half-Jewish Dane who triggers an atomic bomb used against the Japanese on behalf of the Americans, and a loyal German scientist under the Nazis who contributes to the development of atomic weaponry which might have been deployed against the Allies?

13. What do you make of the fact that, unlike most plays, *Copenhagen* makes a virtue of eliminating conventional dramatic indicators including stage directions?

14. According to the author, 'The epistemology of intention is what the play is about' (p. 136). Given the indeterminate nature of its subject matter can he be so sure?

15. How has Frayn designed the play so that a vehicle for ideas becomes an absorbing theatrical experience? You might like to consult reviews of previous productions in considering this question.

16. In what ways does *Copenhagen* bear comparison with either Brecht's *Galileo* or Dürrenmatt's *The Physicist*?

17. 'Everyone remembers the paper – no one remembers the postscript' (p. 69). Do the author's postscripts have anything important to say affecting our understanding and appreciation of the actual play?

18. In the commentary (pp. xvii-xviii) the search for

motivation in *Copenhagen* is compared with Stanislavsky's notion of the super-objective. In what ways might a Stanislavskyan approach to the play help or hinder a performance?

19. In what ways is *Copenhagen*'s contribution to the indeterminacy debate significantly different from the formulation offered by the ancient philosopher Cratylus (a follower of Heraclitus, *c*.540–480 BC) who declared that 'you cannot step twice into the same river'?

20. Why should it be important, for all our sakes, that Heisenberg's unconscious motive for visiting Bohr was, as is suggested at one point in *Copenhagen*, to be 'misunderstood'?

## Methuen Drama Student Editions

Jean Anouilh *Antigone* • John Arden *Serjeant Musgrave's Dance*
Alan Ayckbourn *Confusions* • Aphra Behn *The Rover* • Edward Bond
*Lear* • *Saved* • Bertolt Brecht *The Caucasian Chalk Circle* • *Fear and
Misery in the Third Reich* • *The Good Person of Szechwan* • *Life of Galileo* •
*Mother Courage and her Children* • *The Resistible Rise of Arturo Ui* • *The
Threepenny Opera* • Anton Chekhov *The Cherry Orchard* • *The Seagull* •
*Three Sisters* • *Uncle Vanya* • Caryl Churchill *Serious Money* • *Top Girls*
• Shelagh Delaney *A Taste of Honey* • Euripides *Elektra* • *Medea*•
Dario Fo *Accidental Death of an Anarchist* • Michael Frayn *Copenhagen*
• John Galsworthy *Strife* • Nikolai Gogol *The Government Inspector* •
Robert Holman *Across Oka* • Henrik Ibsen *A Doll's House* • *Ghosts*•
*Hedda Gabler* • Charlotte Keatley *My Mother Said I Never Should* •
Bernard Kops *Dreams of Anne Frank* • Federico García Lorca *Blood
Wedding* • *Doña Rosita the Spinster* (bilingual edition) •*The House of
Bernarda Alba* • (bilingual edition) • *Yerma* (bilingual edition) • David
Mamet *Glengarry Glen Ross* • *Oleanna* • Patrick Marber *Closer* • John
Marston *Malcontent* • Martin McDonagh *The Lieutenant of Inishmore* •
Joe Orton *Loot* • Luigi Pirandello *Six Characters in Search of an Author*
• Mark Ravenhill *Shopping and F\*\*\*ing* • Willy Russell *Blood Brothers*
• *Educating Rita* • Sophocles *Antigone* • *Oedipus the King* • Wole
Soyinka *Death and the King's Horseman* • Shelagh Stephenson *The
Memory of Water* • August Strindberg *Miss Julie* • J. M. Synge *The
Playboy of the Western World* • Theatre Workshop *Oh What a Lovely
War* Timberlake Wertenbaker *Our Country's Good* • Arnold Wesker
*The Merchant* • Oscar Wilde *The Importance of Being Earnest* •
Tennessee Williams *A Streetcar Named Desire* • *The Glass Menagerie*

## Methuen Drama Modern Classics

Jean Anouilh *Antigone* • Brendan Behan *The Hostage* • Robert Bolt
*A Man for All Seasons* • Edward Bond *Saved* • Bertolt Brecht *The
Caucasian Chalk Circle* • *Fear and Misery in the Third Reich* • *The Good
Person of Szechwan* • *Life of Galileo* • *The Messingkauf Dialogues* •
*Mother Courage and Her Children* • *Mr Puntila and His Man Matti* •
*The Resistible Rise of Arturo Ui* • *Rise and Fall of the City of
Mahagonny* • *The Threepenny Opera* • Jim Cartwright *Road* • *Two &
Bed* • Caryl Churchill *Serious Money* • *Top Girls* • Noël Coward
*Blithe Spirit* • *Hay Fever* • *Present Laughter* • *Private Lives* • *The Vortex* •
Shelagh Delancy *A Taste of Honey* • Dario Fo *Accidental Death of an
Anarchist* • Michael Frayn *Copenhagen* • Lorraine Hansberry *A
Raisin in the Sun* • Jonathan Harvey *Beautiful Thing* • David Mamet
*Glengarry Glen Ross* • *Oleanna* • *Speed-the-Plow* • Patrick Marber
*Closer* • *Dealer's Choice* • Arthur Miller *Broken Glass* • Percy Mtwa,
Mbongeni Ngema, Barney Simon *Woza Albert!* • Joe Orton
*Entertaining Mr Sloane* • *Loot* • *What the Butler Saw* • Mark Ravenhill
*Shopping and F***ing* • Willy Russell *Blood Brothers* • *Educating Rita* •
*Stags and Hens* • *Our Day Out* • Jean-Paul Sartre *Crime Passionnel* •
Wole Soyinka • *Death and the King's Horseman* • Theatre Workshop
*Oh, What a Lovely War* • Frank Wedekind • *Spring Awakening* •
Timberlake Wertenbaker *Our Country's Good*